POWERFUL BUDGETING

FOR BETTER PLANNING AND MANAGEMENT

POWERFUL BUDGETING

FOR BETTER PLANNING AND MANAGEMENT

ROBERT G. FINNEY

amacom

American Management Association

New York • Atlanta • Boston • Chicago • Kansas City • San Francisco • Washington, D.C.
Brussels • Toronto • Mexico City

This book is available at a special
discount when ordered in bulk quantities.
For information, contact Special Sales Department,
AMACOM, a division of American Management Association,
135 West 50th Street, New York, NY 10020.

This publication is designed to provide accurate and authoritative information in regard to the subject matter covered. It is sold with the
understanding that the publisher is not engaged in rendering legal,
accounting, or other professional service. If legal advice or other expert assistance is required, the services of a competent professional
person should be sought.

Library of Congress Cataloging-in-Publication Data

Finney, Robert G.
    Powerful budgeting for better planning & management / Robert G.
  Finney.
        p.   cm.
    Includes index.
    ISBN 0-8144-5046-6
    1. Budget in business. I. Title.
HG4028.B8F56   1993
658.15′4—dc20   93-9253
                                                                CIP

Printing number

10   9   8   7   6   5   4   3   2   1

To
Gerald A. Hoyt
Mentor, friend, and outstanding business executive
With gratitude and affection

Contents

Introduction

The annual budget should be a powerful management tool, a company's most useful planning document, but often it is not. There are numerous inherent and man-made problems associated with budgeting that can make it a source of pain rather than satisfaction. In some companies, the budget is treated as a necessary evil. How unfortunate, when it is the one planning/management document that is referred to almost every day in most organizations.

Because almost every manager in every business is involved in budgeting, it should be a valuable management tool; but its importance goes far beyond that. The budget expresses, quantitatively and in detail, what the company plans to do next year and what results it expects. It states how available resources will be employed and deployed and what additional resources will be needed. It communicates where emphasis and priority will be placed and the performance sought. And it supplies this information not in the abstract but in the specifics of people, dollars, equipment, orders, sales, profit, and cash. In short, *the budget is what gives reality to the company's objectives and strategies.*

Good budgeting leads to good management, which leads to good business performance. Not taking advantage of this powerful force for better performance is an unaffordable handicap in any competitive situation. This book presents the approaches, techniques, and practices that will allow any company and any manager to unleash the potential of good budgeting to improve performance.

Budgeting is a management problem, not an accounting problem. Powerful budgeting requires a behavioral approach to a process that develops the best possible information, encourages excellence throughout the company, and overcomes the inherent problems of budgeting. The guiding principle must be "thinking it through before crunching the numbers."

Businesses are characterized both by their differences and by their similarities. Every business has its own unique set of problems and important parameters, but it is equally true that a large body of principles apply to every business. Similar approaches and techniques can be applied beneficially in almost any company in its quest for better budgeting, as long as the company adapts the techniques and processes to its own specific situation.

Nomenclature

The word *budget* means the financial plan of a company for the period of a year, predicting financial results and the contents of the financial statements over that year and predicting in detail the pertinent financial results of all the organization elements of the company. Some companies use other nomenclature, such as *annual operating plan*, but the meaning is the same. (We are not concerned with other types of budgets—individual, government, and so on.) *Budgeting* is the process of preparing budgets.

Budget always means "annual budget." The budget generally matches the annual and quarterly reporting required from a public company, responsive to the fact that the investment community keeps score based on these periods. (Even a private company, if it needs to borrow money or wishes to compare itself with the general world of business and finance, must structure its numbers in the same annual and quarterly increments used by that world.)

Profit, loss, assets, capital, and the like are all used with the usual accounting definitions of the terms. For simplicity, in this book the fiscal year always equals the calendar year.

Businesses take many different organizational forms. In our examples, *company* will always apply to the highest organization under consideration. The top executive of the company will be called the *president*, with apologies to all chief executive officers who are chairmen. Portions of the company for which profit and loss statements are prepared, that is, business entities, will be called *divisions*, and the executive who heads a division will be called the *division general manager* (or DGM). Organizational elements that cannot be described by profit and loss—for instance, design engineering, human resources, eastern region marketing—will be called *functions* or *departments*. There will be frequent reference to *functional managers*, meaning managers at any level who manage functions and thus do not personally have profit-and-loss responsibility.

Organization of the Book

A serious treatment of budgeting must have two quite different objectives: to specify a proper budgeting process and techniques for a business (i.e., a company or division) and to meet the needs of all the functional managers of a business. Functional managers generally have no portfolio to change the budgeting process of their company or division; their needs are to fit into the existing process and get maximum value from budgeting for doing their jobs.

These two objectives are related. When the budgeting process is formulated, the problems of all functional managers at all levels must be understood and addressed, and the resulting techniques must be applicable to all levels. Functional managers are both budgeting participants and the best source of direct knowledge about company operations. Regarding the other objective, it is useful for functional managers to learn good principles and practice in a subject as important to them as budgeting. It allows them to put their budgeting work in the context of what business budgeting is all about and what their companies are trying to accomplish through their budgets.

Of particular concern are functional managers who are in a bad budgeting situation. It is all well and good to describe the process and techniques of a powerful budgeting process, but what is the relevance to lower-level functional managers caught in a poor budgeting process that they have no authority to change?

In fact, functional managers caught in a poor budgeting process can do quite a bit. They can improve their own budgets, they can influence their superiors and neighbor departments to adopt more valuable budgets, and sometimes they can be the driving force for improved budgeting for their division or company. In other words, they can replace some of their budgeting pain and frustration with satisfaction. They can develop a tool that will help them do their own jobs better while protecting them against irrationality elsewhere by using the same techniques of powerful budgeting applicable to the company, although the details and constraints will be different. Thus, any discussion of powerful budgeting must include ways for a functional manager to apply these techniques and obtain value in a deficient budgeting environment.

These objectives and concerns are addressed in the following ways. The main organization of the book is a presentation of principles and practices, approaches and techniques for powerful budgeting for an entire business; they thus benefit managers at all levels. The concerns and problems of functional managers fall naturally into the discussion, because they are essential participants in the process. For example, Chapter 4, "Objectives of the Budgeting Process," includes the budgeting objectives of a functional manager. In Chapter 5, "Inherent Problems to Overcome," the discussion under "Psychology" applies equally to functional managers and top management.

Additionally, the sequence is interrupted frequently to address what a functional manager can do to overcome a bad budgeting environment. Such problem-addressing sections are found at the ends of Chapters 6 through 12. They are all entitled "Functional Managers: Surmounting a Poor Budgeting Process" to identify them as specifically directed at this subject. The section at the end of Chapter 6 deals with whether and when a functional manager should attempt to change the company's budgeting process and with how to influence neighbor departments toward better budgeting. The sections at the ends of Chapters 7 through 11 treat the application of the technique discussed in the chapter by examining a functional manager caught in a poor process. The section at the end of Chapter 12 covers a private, local budgeting process that should be used by a functional manager in the same situation. The contents are thus organized to present the total subject of powerful budgeting logically, while ensuring that functional managers' particular problems are addressed at appropriate points in the flow.

Finally, regarding functional managers, it is generally assumed that the reader has had some experience with budgeting. However, for those who have not, the Appendix, "A New Manager's First Budget," is included. The Appendix is written for the manager who has no familiarity with budgeting. It discusses what to expect and how he or she should approach a first budget. It is suggested that readers encountering budgeting for the first time read the Appendix first; it is a useful introduction to the subject.

Part I, "Addressing the Objectives and Obstacles," begins with an overview of powerful budgeting. The fictitious QRS Company is then used to illustrate common budgeting problems and deficiencies. This is followed by a discussion of what the QRS budget should have been in order to improve business performance. With this background of problems and a solution, the objectives of the various budgeting participants are developed, and the inherent obstacles to good budgeting are discussed. Reasoning from these objectives and obstacles, Part I ends with the requirements that a budgeting process must meet for the budget to fulfill its potential as a powerful planning and management tool.

Part II, "Satisfying the Requirements," presents the techniques that result in good budgets. Chapters 7 through 11 cover, respectively, techniques for establishing the context, dealing with uncertainty, selecting the format, developing the content, and encouraging excellence. Chapter 12 puts it all together with the proper process flow and organization of details needed to ensure accuracy, consistency, and proper communication. Chapter 12 also treats the transition from current practices to powerful budgeting techniques.

Although the entire budgeting process outlined is recommended, value will be obtained by implementing any of the techniques; each one can be introduced independently of the others. While "all" is better than "some," better budgeting is not an "all or nothing" proposition.

Part I

Addressing the Objectives and Obstacles

1

Overview:
From Pain to Power

Business managers are generally smart, aggressive, and results-oriented. Give them a problem and they will attack it with vigor. When you say, "Let's prepare next year's budget," however, their behavior often appears to be irrational.

Pain and Limited Usefulness

There are things in every budgeting process that make it less than satisfying for both the person seeking budget approval (the submitter) and the person who has to approve it (the reviewer). (Everyone involved except the lowest-level manager and the board of directors plays both the submitter and reviewer roles.) To start with, budgeting is a multidimensional guessing game. The submitters have to guess, to a degree, what the reviewer wants to see in the budget and what he or she will accept. At the same time, they usually have strong feelings about what they can accomplish and what they will need. Can they afford a straightforward presentation, or will they be subject to an arbitrary cut in any case? If they believe the latter, they will, of course, pad their submission by the expected amount of the cut.

From the reviewer's point of view, he or she must decide whether the submitter is an optimist or a pessimist. Does the person regularly meet budget commitments? A very profitable, very successful division reporting to me at one time protested at every budget review that both competition and technology were going

3

to hurt them severely, and they would be lucky if profits did not decrease 50 percent in the coming year; their revenue would decline, but they would need large increases in both development and marketing expenses to survive. In fact, every year while I was involved, the profit grew; twelve years later, this business is still operating quite successfully.

Such superpessimists illustrate another problem: Bonus payments are often tied to performance vis-à-vis budget. There are good reasons for this, but a guaranteed result is increased game playing in the budgeting process. It is difficult to get intelligent people to act against their own self-interest, and that self-interest is clearly the lowest-profit or highest-expense budget they can get approved.

A major source of budgeting pain for the participants is that budgets tend to be "cast in concrete." That semifictitious budget will haunt them all year, and they probably will not be able to escape from the numbers on those pages.

Both the timing of the budgeting process and the amount of time spent on it add to the pain and limit its usefulness. Boards of directors generally approve budgets in December. The amount of work required and the multiple levels of organizational hierarchy usually require that the budgeting process start no later than September. Some corporations begin earlier than that. This long lead time both prolongs the intrinsic pain of the process and makes the prediction worse, because the prediction is for fifteen months (or more) hence, not twelve.

Finally, there is another time problem, reflected in the adage, "There is never enough time to do it right, but always time to do it over." The cycle of multiple reviews and consolidations as the budget proceeds toward the board of directors carries time pressure at each step. Seldom do managers allocate the time for enough analysis and reflection until some time during the year when results are so far off budget that excruciating analysis begins.

So we have a process on which managers busily spend at least a quarter of the year, and whose results are often demonstrably wrong by the end of January. Is it not strange that these managers put up with this? Should stockholders have a warm feeling about a budget generated in such a fashion, particularly when it is going to be the basis of much of management's actions for the coming year?

The Power of Budgeting

Budgeting *can* be the vehicle for addressing objectives, strategies, and problems in the most intelligent way. It *should* be the vehicle which gives reality to the company's objectives and strategies and should reflect the organization's considered decisions on strategy, courses of action, and responses to problems. Further, it should consistently communicate all these things to the entire organization. Finally, it is the *only* vehicle that can accomplish all these things, because it expresses the decisions, responses, and actions with numerical specificity in relation to time and is subsequently used to measure the performance of the company and its component departments. The budget is *the* most important planning document of the company.

Because the budget is used both to express the company's plans numerically and later to measure performance, it should be a powerful management tool. It should guide and motivate the company toward the best performance possible in its ever-changing environment. It should assist all levels of management in timely recognition and reaction to the surprises and problems that all companies experience. And it should promulgate to all employees the all-important message that "management knows what it is doing." Good budgeting leads to good management, which leads to good business performance.

To accomplish these goals, one must approach budgeting as a management process, not as a financial or arithmetic exercise. The budgeting objectives and the obstacles (inherent problems) to good budgeting must be determined. A budgeting process and budgeting techniques must then be carefully chosen so that the objectives are addressed and the obstacles neutralized. Managers must adopt the mind-set that the budget is primarily a *plan* of actions and desired accomplishments, not just a prediction of results. Further, they must recognize that numerous important factors that affect results are beyond the company's control and provide a mechanism for facilitating changes of plans when necessary.

The problems of budgeting do not result from stupidity or contrariness of the participants. Business managers generally are highly intelligent and highly motivated and will work hard for a worthwhile result. The objectives of budgeting vary from participant to participant, however, and some of them conflict. Every company must overcome this problem and others inherent in budgeting. The task, then, is to reason from the objectives and obstacles to a set of budgeting requirements that will meet the former and neutralize the latter and to design a process and implement techniques that meet these requirements.

Budgeting Objectives and Obstacles

The superficial purpose of the budgeting process is to predict the results of the following year. In reality, however, there are a number of valid objectives, and the problem is that they differ from participant to participant. The single owner of a business wants a budget that plans the best profit realistically achievable; the main concern of the lowest-level functional managers is to know what is expected of them and to be given enough resources to accomplish it.

To be successful, the budgeting process must be responsive to the needs of *all* participants. Fortunately the goals of the different participants are similar enough that a realistic composite set of objectives can be formulated and used as a basis for budgeting requirements. These composite objectives are a budget that:

- Is realistic, accurate, and consistent
- Plans the best results achievable consistent with acceptable risk and long-term health
- Contains the information most useful to management
- Is consistent with strategy
- Facilitates goal setting and measurement at all levels
- Communicates strategy, plans, and required outputs to the organization
- Communicates operating plans across functions

- Will be beaten
- Will be approved
- Gives every department the resources it needs to meet its budget

Unfortunately, there is a significant conflict between two of the budgeting objectives: the contradiction between planning "the best results achievable" and a budget that "will be beaten." This conflict of objectives is the first of the inherent problems, the budgeting obstacles that are fundamental to the activity of budgeting and cannot be avoided or removed. Other inherent problems are that performance is *measured* against the budget, the future is uncertain, the outside environment is uncontrollable, and budgeting is fundamentally a psychological process.

The fundamental problem of budgeting can be summarized from the obstacles. The budget deals with next year. Many things about next year are uncertain because (1) it is in the future, and (2) much of it is uncontrollable. Of the part that can be known, the people who know best—the functional managers directly on the firing line—are not motivated to be realistic in their budgeting submissions. The finished budget is then (usually) cast in concrete and (always) used to measure the participants.

Reasoning from these composite objectives and inherent obstacles yields six requirements that must be met for budgeting to fulfill its potential:

1. The budget must be prepared in the proper strategic context, firmly within the framework of the objectives, strategies, and plans of the company.
2. The process must deal realistically with uncertainty and uncontrollability.
3. The format that provides the most useful information for management must be selected.
4. The content must provide the best possible numerical predictions of the next year's results.
5. The process must emphasize encouragement of excellence at all levels of the company.
6. A coherent, efficient, and timely process flow must tie everything together.

These requirements must be met throughout the company, at all levels of management.

Functional Managers: Surmounting a Poor Budgeting Process

Before discussing how to satisfy these requirements, it is appropriate to consider the options of functional managers caught in a poor budgeting process. As stated in the Introduction, they have quite a few. First, their budgeting, job performance, and satisfaction will increase merely from understanding how powerful the budgeting process can be, even if they do not have the authority to institute such a process.

Second, the functional manager can apply the techniques of powerful budgeting to his or her own budget. Each of the techniques is applicable to any function and will improve its budgeting. The techniques require a different perspective, however, when applied to a function as opposed to an entire company. Their application by a functional manager is covered at the end of each of the following discussions of budgeting techniques and process. For easy identification, the pertinent paragraphs all start, *"A functional manager caught in a poor budgeting process. . . ."*

Third, the functional manager can influence neighbor departments toward better budgeting. The work of different functions is so intertwined that the effects of good budgeting increase significantly as good practices broaden. This has to be done by example and persuasion. Persuasion is most effective when the functional manager sets a good example by using good budgeting himself or herself. The functional manager generally starts by asking for inputs and help in carrying out the various budgeting techniques. By setting an example and involving superiors and peers, the functional manager can demonstrate the benefits of powerful budgeting to them, leading, one hopes, to acceptance and advocacy. (A good time to advocate improved budgeting is when major changes, like cost reductions, must be made; the anguish of such major changes makes managers receptive to a fresh approach.)

Fourth, under the right circumstances the functional manager can make, and be recognized for, a significant contribution to the company by spearheading the drive to powerful budgeting. However, the functional manager should undertake such an initiative *if and only if* top management is demonstrably unhappy with current practice and believes in the importance of good budgeting, he or she has enough prestige to cause peers and superiors to follow his or her lead, and accounting will not fight the change.

Satisfying the Requirements

Each of the six budgeting requirements must be attacked with deliberate techniques, which together comprise a coherent and fulfilling process.

Establishing the Context

To place the budget in its proper strategic context, a planning continuum must be established leading from objectives and strategy through to the finished budget. Content and timing must be integrated at every step.

Four items must be incorporated in the budgeting process to establish the planning continuum: (1) the important outside environmental factors (OEFs), (2) the critical factors for success and related concerns, (3) a summary (one-page) strategy statement, and (4) the preliminary budget numbers.

OEFs are factors beyond the company's control that have an important bearing on its results. To be useful in budgeting, the identified OEFs must be specific and capable of quantification, and a relationship between their changes and business results must be demonstrable. Each company will have a different list, although the OEFs of direct competitors will ordinarily be similar. To be specific, they must be developed in an inside-out process, starting, for example, with expense and reasoning to the uncontrollable outside factors (such as material prices) that have important effects on expense.

The critical factors for success and related considerations become the focus for the action plans that must underlie the budget.

The summary one-page strategy is a statement of priorities and emphasis by the president and should include both what the company will do and what it will not do. The best way to accomplish consistency in numbers is to use the strategic projections for the next year as the preliminary budget.

Strategic planning is a broad subject beyond the scope of this book. The point for budgeting is that these four items are required as inputs; if not done in strategic planning, they must be done as the first step in the budgeting process.

A functional manager caught in a poor budgeting process also needs a context for the function's budget and must establish his or her own. The functional manager's context is not only company strategy but also division strategy and the goals, plans, and desires of superiors. The search for this strategy/management context should concentrate on things that directly affect the function, reasoning from the function's outputs and cost drivers to the needs, desires, and strategies of superiors, the division, and the company. If not known, they must be sought from superiors; if not found, explicit assumptions should be made.

Dealing With Uncertainty and Uncontrollability

When budgets are made up indiscriminately of items that management can control and items beyond its control, it becomes impossible to tell whether management is doing a good job or is just lucky or unlucky. The assumptions process is recommended for dealing with uncertainty and factors beyond the company's control.

The assumptions process (1) identifies the important OEFs, (2) makes an assumption about each one, (3) develops budget numbers based on these assumptions, (4) reviews these assumptions over the course of the year, and (5) changes the budget if and when it becomes clear that the assumptions should be changed. This process yields many benefits, not the least of which is allowing managers to be measured separately on performance and on their reaction to uncontrollable changes.

To be useful, the assumptions must be specific, quantified, and at the right level of specificity to represent a meaningful cause-and-effect relationship. They follow directly from the identified OEFs and must be company-specific. Care must be taken that the assumptions are neither so general as to be useless (for instance, "There will be a recession") nor so presumptuous that they assume away management's job (for example, "Next year's orders budget will be met"). They must relate directly to pertinent OEFs and to the business.

The assumptions process, and particularly changes in assumptions during the year, requires a disinterested review board to ensure that the assumptions represent genuine uncontrollable factors and are not being used to excuse poor performance. The board of directors, with its general experience and broad perspective, is ideally suited for this role. An important side benefit is that this is a particularly appropriate way for the board to increase its knowledge of the company and the value of its contribution.

A functional manager caught in a poor budgeting process can use the assumptions process with the same benefits that it confers on the company. In contrast with a company, a function controls few of the determinants of its input and output. Therefore, in addition to OEFs, functional assumptions are appropriate for internal uncontrollable factors (IUFs). (Care must be taken not to include as IUFs matters that the function is supposed to influence as part of its responsibility, such as plans and actions of the department or division within which it resides.) Functional managers, together with key people and superiors if conditions permit, should reason from function inputs and outputs to important OEFs and IUFs, make assumptions for these, and state the assumptions as a prominent part of budget submission and review. Unfortunately, in a poor budgeting process changed assumptions will not be accepted as a reason for budget relief, but the functional manager can still use them to develop understanding by superiors regarding what is uncontrollable about the function's work.

Selecting the Format

The most useful information for management is that which best portrays the benefits and consequences of its activities and actions. This must be addressed in selecting the budget format because the periodic reports used to manage the business should be in the same format as the budget. To provide the most useful information for management, the budget format must (1) emphasize profit and cash flow directly, (2) focus on total costs, rather than burdens (i.e., costs allocated to other costs in particular proportions, such as administrative expense allocated to a product in proportion to sales) and ratios, and (3) relate business outputs to *activities.*

Traditional methods often obscure rather than clarify these things. Most burden rates and ratios (1) assign costs based on a gross parameter that is not the driver of those costs and (2) apply the charges related to one product to the profitability of another.

A step in the right direction is to base the budget format on fixed and variable costs, a process often called "flexible budgeting." This approach assigns only the variable costs associated with a product to that product. Fixed costs, those that do not vary with sales, are treated separately. Flexible budgeting yields a number of advantages over traditional methods: a direct measure of product profitability, knowledge of the fixed costs of the business, information concerning whether the company is a high-fixed-cost or high-variable-cost business, and a focus on the appropriateness of incremental pricing.

The major imperfection of flexible budgeting is that it does not assign fixed or indirect costs to products or services. There is nothing fundamental or magical about the distinction between direct and indirect costs. Indeed, as businesses of all kinds implement more automation, indirect costs become proportionally larger and more variable. For a totally automated factory, direct labor cost would be zero, so traditional methods could not allocate "indirect labor" to products.

Activity-based costing (ABC) is a mechanism that can potentially relate all costs directly to the products or services that cause them. It is a cost management system that relates all work activity of a company to its outputs. The cost drivers of each activity are defined and used to assign costs to products shipped and services rendered. Implementing ABC can be a major challenge, because people are being asked to think in a very different way and because it can be difficult to identify the cost drivers with satisfying precision. For these reasons, partial implementation of ABC—for all indirect costs—is the best solution for many companies. Even imperfect or partial steps toward ABC will give a company a better understanding of the profitability of different products and services.

Assignment of general and administrative (G&A) and corporate costs to divisions, products, and services has some special problems. However, assigning such costs on an activity basis, rather than in accordance with sales or cost of sales, not only makes budgeting more valuable but also can be a major tool in strategic analysis.

A functional manager caught in a poor budgeting process is probably required to use a format that is not the most useful for him or her. He or she should decide which parameters are most useful and develop a private budget format in those terms, maintaining and tracking it on a personal-computer spreadsheet. Some information may not be readily available, but some improvements undoubtedly will be both worth doing and easy to do. The functional manager must pay close attention to the company's budget format but should keep his or her superior informed of the private budget form and explain problems and good results in its terms whenever possible. The private form, after all, emphasizes the parameters most important to the function.

Developing the Content

The budget deals with the unknown future, and the numbers that express expected performance for next year are necessarily estimates. The task is to make sure these numerical entries are the most probable and meaningful that they can be.

There are only three sources of budgeting estimates: data, trends, and models. The problems that cause the reliability of the budget's numerical content to deteriorate are mainly the misuse of these sources, e.g., stretching data beyond the time when it is meaningful or either blindly following trends or ignoring them.

The most difficult and critical numerical predictions are those of sales. The problems of predicting sales are quite different in different kinds of businesses; in some, sales follow from orders, while in others (e.g., a cash retail business) orders have no meaning. Some businesses rely on a few large orders or sales, while others have many small orders or sales. The latter type of business can use probability and statistics, models, and questioned trends (external trends must always be questioned, never blindly followed) to predict sales. The business in which individual orders have no meaning *must* use them. The "large but few sales" business, on the other hand, can get little value from statistics or trends, because each order is critical. This type of business must use data on specific prospects as far ahead in time as is valid, and should use a model beyond that point in time.

Predicting costs constitutes the bulk of the number-crunching work of budgeting. The first key to good cost prediction is again the proper use of data, trends, and models. The second key is to base cost prediction on a firm understanding of organization activities, outputs, and cost drivers and the relationships between them.

The use of mathematical modeling is essential to good budgeting, and beyond that it is useful for understanding and managing a business or a function. Good value can be obtained from simple models, done on personal computers using spreadsheet programs, if the limitations of the model are understood. A relatively simple model for an entire business is useful as a generator of a preliminary budget and for analysis of alternatives.

A functional manager caught in a poor budgeting process can directly apply all aspects of proper use of data, trends, models, and input/output relationships. The functional manager obviously must be responsive to superiors' desires. If data or trend support for numbers is inappropriately demanded, the functional manager should still ensure that the numbers were developed properly and attempt to steer reviews toward the proper use of the three sources of budget numbers.

Encouraging Excellence

Management owes the owner(s) the best possible performance that can be planned. But because all the inherent problems are arrayed against this objective, a deliberate technique is needed to encourage excellence at all levels. An effective technique to accomplish this goal is gap analysis.

Gap analysis begins with identifying a parameter of concern or interest (orders, skill level, factory rework level, profit, and so forth) called the gap dimension. The desired goal level for this parameter is projected, as is the expected status quo result, i.e., the result of continuing to do the same things in the same way. The difference between these two projections defines a *gap*. The all-important final step is to develop action programs to fill the gap.

The beauty of gap analysis lies in the many ways it can be applied, while giving all participants a common language in which to deal objectively with goals, problems, and actions. It can be used at all levels for all types of problems and improvements as long as the dimension is specific and one the organization can change by its actions.

Gap analysis is used in budgeting to decide on and plan for the most important actions throughout the company for the next year. An organization should do only a small number of gap analyses; the purpose is to focus the organization's attention on important results, and too many would defocus it.

There is management value in negative information (gaps that cannot be filled). Gap analysis can help identify these problems and clarify the proper goals for an organization. It is also a good tool for solving multifunction problems.

A functional manager caught in a poor budgeting process can effectively use gap analysis, which is useful at all levels of the company, for a wide variety of problems. In this situation, the functional manager probably should use the status quo result, rather than the goal, for the budget numbers, depending on the situation. For example, if the superior always attacks the manager's numbers, the goal numbers should be kept in reserve to fulfill the expected demand for improvement.

Process Flow and the Details

The last budgeting requirement is that everything be tied together in a process that flows coherently and includes all the details in an effective and efficient manner. This is a two-stage operation.

The first stage is "thinking it through." The inputs are existing sales backlog, the one-page strategy statement, the identified OEFs, and selected gap dimensions. (In addition, there are some generalized inputs to both stages: administrative directions, models, and budget format.) The main output of the first stage is a preliminary budget, which serves to (1) indicate whether chosen alternatives will yield a satisfactory budget and (2) provide direction for the detailed work of the second stage. Quantifying the gaps for the chosen gap dimensions is also a first-stage output. Ideally, a fair amount of the first-stage budgeting work will have been done during strategic planning.

The second and final stage involves "crunching the numbers," generating all the details of the final budgets for all departments. The inputs are the outputs of the first stage plus the generalized inputs. The second-stage output is the approved final budget for the next year.

The details of the budgeting process must be carefully organized to ensure accuracy, consistency, and communication throughout the organization. Number crunching should be made as automatic as possible to avoid the error inherent in manipulating a large mass of numbers, and specific responsibility and procedures should be assigned for keeping a strict trail of revisions. The two main communication concerns are that every necessary interaction be covered consistently and that all elements of cost for a given activity be included. Clearly designating a capable budget analyst with coordination responsibility and relying on the accounting department in general are good ways to promote the required communication.

Again, while this entire process of powerful budgeting is recommended, incremental value will be obtained from implementing any one of the recommended techniques. The value and difficulty of implementing different techniques depends on the culture, sophistication, and problems of a company. In general, however, some are easy (flexible budgeting), some are difficult (the assumptions process), some lend themselves to experimentation (activity-based costing), and some can be done independently of anything else (spreadsheet programs). Different techniques yield different benefits; the assumptions process aids strategic management, gap analysis aids operations and problem solving, and so on. The preferred approach, the most aggressive, is to plan and announce a multiyear program to replace budgeting pain with power, including phases of experimentation, partial implementation, and partial results.

A functional manager caught in a poor budgeting process needs a logical private process to generate the needed information in a timely manner relative to the company's budgeting process. Before the company's process begins, the functional manager should identify three things (fortunately, each is a major effort only once): the function's output dictators and cost drivers, the pertinent outside environmental factors and internal uncontrollable factors, and the private-budget format. In addition, gap analysis for the selected budgeting dimension should be conducted early in the function's budgeting process. Poor budgeting processes are characterized by unrealistic time pressure on functional managers, so they should schedule the private process so that the "thinking it through" work is done before the company's number crunching begins in earnest.

Business Benefits From Powerful Budgeting

This book gives numerous examples of possibly surprising ways in which good budgeting can contribute directly to better business performance: by serving as an aid in downsizing, in assimilating a new acquisition, and in better pricing, among others. Good budgeting provides the information, focus, and assured attitude required for good major decisions, excellence and control in all activities, and intelligent and timely reaction to problems and surprises. Properly handling the uncertainty of the future and the uncontrollability of OEFs is probably the greatest contribution to better business results. The final business benefit of good budgeting is the better results that will follow from improved motivation and morale of the entire company.

2

Illustrating the Problems: The QRS Company Budget

In this chapter, common budgeting problems are illustrated by considering the budgeting process of the fictitious QRS Company, a public entity with about $200 million in sales. QRS makes, sells, and services instrumentation used in engineering and test laboratories of government and industry. Some years ago, both technologies and markets diverged enough that QRS was organized into semiautonomous divisions, called Growth, Service, New, and Mature.

> *Growth Division:* Makes and sells data acquisition instrumentation
>
> *Service Division:* Services a variety of instrumentation, for the federal government only, by choice
>
> *New Division:* Acquired during the current year; makes and sells medical instrumentation products
>
> *Mature Divison:* Makes and sells specialized instrumentation computers that are slowly but surely being replaced by more versatile, cheaper, general-purpose computers

QRS has been steadily profitable but without much growth, and the return on investment has not been spectacular. The company develops an annual calendar-year budget in September through November for presentation to the board of directors in December.

The president of QRS is the chief executive officer, responsible to a board of outside directors. Like most such boards, the QRS directors are intelligent and experienced but, spending about a day a month on QRS business, are not really knowledgeable about that business. The directors are mainly supportive of the president, but a couple have their own strong ideas about different directions QRS should take. They all have some reservations about an acquisition that the president got them to approve this year, the New Division. The directors focus on profit and return on investment and expect both to be higher next year. They are currently concerned about deteriorating gross margins.

Let's follow the budgeting process through the four divisions and then kibitz on the final preparation and presentation of the corporate budget to the board.

Growth Division

Growth Division is a profitable and growing data acquisition products business, but the division general manager (DGM) has problems. Two years ago Growth prepared a five-year projection, which promised 15 percent profit growth per year. Owing to unforeseen economic problems in Growth's market, profit so far has been well below that projected, and return on investment has been low. The DGM knows that material costs are increasing but that he cannot raise prices and therefore is facing lower gross margins. He believes that he cannot cut indirect expenses without hurting sales and quality; indeed, he believes he must increase indirect expenses to protect the current level of sales.

The DGM knows that the president and the board remember the two-year-old projection, focus on return on investment, and expect more profit next year. He also knows that they consider gross margin quite important and have been pressuring the divisions to increase it. The DGM also strongly believes that his engineering department has a great new product idea that can get Growth back on its growth track by the third year hence, but pursuing that product correctly will severely lower next year's profit.

Concerned for his job and knowing the president's needs and biases, the DGM convinces himself that he can get a major increase in orders for the coming year (without a convincing plan or increased sales expense). He knows that his sales manager is overoptimistic, and he usually cuts the latter's sales projections, but this year the DGM accepts it without modification. (He gets a certain satisfaction from this. He tells himself, "Okay, that son of a gun hung his tail out again this year, but I am not going to protect him this time.") This higher orders forecast lets him add some indirect expense and still show accelerating profit growth. He adds half the indirect expense and half the development expense he thinks he needs.

When presented with Growth's budget, the president thinks, "Good, finally orders will be on track." He does not modify the revenue projection but cuts indirect and development expense by a small, arbitrary amount.

The result is that reality has not been addressed. The president is happy, momentarily. The DGM is uncomfortable. He puts himself in a defensive frame of mind, resolves to keep unremitting pressure on the sales manager, and hopes he gets lucky.

A Customer Service Manager in Growth Division

The customer service managers (functional managers) are on the firing line, the focal point for customer complaints. Often, whether a customer is satisfied and will buy more of Growth's products depends on the quality of customer service's work. As Growth's business has increased, the customer service managers (CSMs) have worked longer and longer hours to keep up with the increasing work load.

One CSM knows that Growth's DGM intellectually understands that she needs more people, but the DGM's whole emphasis this year seems to be on holding costs down. The DGM says, "You will have to work smarter." The CSM feels that her people have continually worked smarter and that there are very few productivity gains to be made in the short term.

The CSM decides that she must be aggressive. She prepares a persuasive (somewhat exaggerated) presentation explaining the importance and the growth of her organization's work. She submits a budget with 20 percent growth in cost over the current year. As expected, in a long review, the DGM cuts her to 10 percent growth, which is what she wanted in the first place.

However, her satisfaction is short-lived. When the president makes his small, arbitrary cuts in the DGM's budget, the DGM decides that new-product development is the most important item on his agenda, so he has to cut elsewhere. Therefore, he takes the entire 10 percent expense increase out of the CSM's budget and refuses to listen to protests.

The CSM is not happy with the prospect of facing the long hours and screaming customers of next year resulting from no increase in expenses.

Service Division

The DGM of the Service Division is highly regarded in QRS; she has achieved a steady 10 percent growth and excellent return on investment for the past three years. She is a compulsive commitment meeter, and she insists that her people have this same dedication to meeting commitments. One result is that every level of her organization pads its budgets, including the DGM, so Service's budget ends up with "pads" on top of "pads."

But the DGM of Service also has some problems in putting together her budget. This year, with the blessing of the president, she doubled her sales force to increase future growth in this high-return business, reducing current profit. The division sells a service to the federal government, which has repeated year after year with less than 5 percent lost sales annually. This year, however, changes in government procurement practice have suddenly increased the number of contracts not renewed. The DGM believes that this lost business will continue, that she will need her increased sales force to have any growth at all, and that she must add proposal-writing expense. The president is aware of the lost-business problem but believes that it is a one-time event. He still expects the increased sales force to yield 15 percent growth next year.

Without first discussing it with the president, the DGM submits a budget that shows a small decrease in sales and profit from the current year. She tells the president that the procurement ground rules have definitely changed, making the current mode of operating much less attractive. It will take a year to see if the lost-business trend continues and to develop the right new marketing methods and, perhaps, new markets. Meanwhile, she cannot commit to better results.

The president is very unhappily surprised. He expected a growth budget, a payoff from the increased sales force. He knows the DGM is compulsive about meeting her commitments and therefore believes she is again just being conservative in her budgeting. Further, in QRS the DGM bonuses are primarily based on profit relative to budget, so the president is continually on the alert for sandbagged budgets and tends to pressure all of them upward.

The president browbeats the DGM to increase the profit in her budget, but the DGM resists. After two emotional, half-day meetings, the president demands a budget with 7.5 percent profit growth. The DGM submits a budget with higher orders and sales, less lost business, and expenses cut below the current year's level.

Both the president and the DGM are dissatisfied. The DGM feels committed only to "her" submitted budget, not to the president's budget. Further, the DGM feels she has been treated unfairly, since her budget is the strongest determinant of her bonus.

The Material Manager in the Service Division

The material manager of Service has conscientiously worked hard all year on the problem of reducing repair costs for equipment the division maintains. He has concluded that an in-house repair facility for selected modules would increase expense next year but result in significantly reduced expense after that. A month before the start of the budgeting process, he received the DGM's approval to begin spending money for the facility in January. He has done the detailed planning and has put the increased expense for next year in his budget.

The DGM approves his budget without change in the first review. However, after the president cuts the Service expense, the DGM tells the material manager to cancel the plans for the in-house repair facility. Further, the material manager has to cut expenses below this year's level. Since increasing outside repair costs were the problem in the first place, and since the budget now shows increased sales, the material manager does not know how to live with reduced expenses.

The DGM blames the problem on the president and tells the material manager, "Do the best you can." The material manager is demotivated, to say the least.

New Division

The New Division was acquired during the current year, with only lukewarm support of the board. The DGM was the CEO of this business when it was independent, although not a major stockholder (that is, he did not get rich in the acquisition).

Last spring the DGM of New presented optimistic projections for his business as part of the acquisition process, trying to get the best price for its (then) owners. Now he does not believe that he can meet those projections next year. Also, he has no idea how the president reacts to budgets—for instance, does he always make arbitrary cuts? Finally, he feels that the supporting information ordered by the corporate controller is voluminous, misleading, and irrelevant. He has to spend so much time during the budgeting process complying with this demand for supporting information that he feels he has not carried out *his* normal budget process satisfactorily.

Because of the uncertainty of the president's reaction to budgets, the time required to gather and prepare the voluminous data for the controller, and his desire to be let alone, New's DGM decides to "punt" and submits a budget that is approximately equal to the acquisition projections.

The president, knowing he is under the gun on this acquisition, is relieved. He tries to review this budget exhaustively, but he does not yet understand New or the medical instrumentation business in depth. The review gravitates so strongly to the supporting data—errors, misunderstandings, ratios so different from those of the other divisions, and so on—that the president does not reach the essence of the problems. In the end, the president approves the budget without change.

Chances are that these budget projections will be missed; by midyear there will probably be a loss of credibility of this DGM with the president, and of the president with the board of directors.

The Western Region Sales Manager in the New Division

New's western region sales manager is confused during the budgeting process. She cannot seem to get the attention of the DGM or the sales manager (her boss), and she has not received a normal reaction to her budget submission. She knows her region well, believes that her submission of small growth in orders next year is a challenge, and expects recognition for accepting the challenge unbidden.

There has always been a distance problem and a "field versus headquarters" attitude in New, but this year it is worse. Rather than reactions to her budget, initially she keeps getting requests for more supporting information that she does not understand. Then, suddenly she receives the edict that she must budget more orders and that a higher proportion must come early in the year.

She tries to argue her case on the phone and on a trip to headquarters. Her boss is sympathetic, but she gets nowhere. She finally gives up and submits the requested orders budget. She has been concerned about the future as part of QRS; if this is any indication, she decides, the acquisition by QRS will be bad for New.

Mature Division

Mature is a large but declining business. Its marching orders have been to run out the business as long and as profitably as possible, but not to invest.

The DGM of Mature has a continual battle to downsize his organization intelligently and to maintain acceptable morale while doing so. He often comments that if the division were growing to the current level of sales, it would do things more simply and with less expense than it does now. Having fallen from a higher level instead, the organization tends to believe that at least one of all the specialized people and procedures is needed.

The manager of Mature's administration department knows that he is expected to cut people in his budget submission. However, he has twenty-five years with the company, and most of his subordinates are also old hands. He believes every bit of work his organization does is essential and cannot face cutting any of these people. He develops elaborate justifications for work that requires just the number of personnel currently employed by the organization. He then severely cuts the supporting expenses (telephone, travel, information services) his people need to do that work. The DGM reviews his budget, argues with him without changing the manager's position, and finally says that he, the DGM, will cut the administration department budget himself if the manager cannot. The DGM, the manager, and the division controller spend a whole day cutting the budget. At the end, the DGM is pleased with the logic of the cuts, comfortable with the result, but worried about the manager's morale. Subsequently, he is surprised that the administration manager's morale is good; the administration manager understood deep down that cuts were needed, and he is relieved that he was able to pass the buck to the DGM to make the tough decisions.

The manager of the marketing department represents a different problem. He is a man who knows all the buzzwords and liberally uses platitudes, for example, the marketing budget should increase when sales are poor. He is on a crusade to turn Mature around and submits a budget that doubles his expense to lead that crusade. The DGM has given clear direction, wonders why the marketing manager does not understand that direction, and further believes that the marketing manager is too shallow to lead any crusade. The DGM summarily rejects any expense increase, but the marketing manager wears him down so much during the long budget review that he finally accepts a budget expense equal to the current year's. The DGM's plan before the review was to cut marketing expense by 15 percent, so now he has to tighten the screws further on his other departments.

The Mature budget submitted to the president is finally a summation of compromises, representing a plan to do things essentially the same way but somehow cheaper. The president decrees an additional arbitrary expense cut in the Mature budget and challenges the DGM to find where those cuts can be made while still optimizing the runout of the business.

The DGM of Mature sees a big hill to climb in front of him and does not know quite how to go about it.

The Corporate QRS Budget

The president and the corporate controller consolidate these division budgets into the corporate budget and prepare to present it to the board of directors. The president believes that he has the support of the board but that they are wary about the acquisition of New and expect an increase in profit next year.

He has the Growth budget, which shows that division getting back on its growth track. He is angry about the Service budget but expects that division to achieve some profit growth. He believes strongly in New's business and appreciates its budget, although he is a bit uneasy about his personal lack of understanding it in depth. He is relatively comfortable about Mature's budget, knowing that the DGM will work hard and do the best he can.

So the president is relatively happy. Without New, the budget predicts a profit increase over this year. The addition of a full year of New results, as opposed to partial-year proceeds for the current year, makes it a nice, upbeat budget. The president believes that the board will be pleased and docile. Because he has been around the block a few times and because his bonus is also mostly dependent on actual profit results vis-à-vis budget figures, the president adds a sizable pad to corporate expense and declares the budget final.

During the board's review, only three topics receive lengthy discussion. The first is, "Why don't we pour money into Mature and turn it around?" One director who particularly remembers the past glory of Mature believes it is shameful to just let it run out; however, the rest of the board and the president agree that Mature's time is past. The second lengthy discussion is about the smallest item in the capital budget: refurbishment of the boardroom. Two directors believe that the boardroom is fine and that this item represents a waste of money. The president argues that the boardroom is the main place for meetings with customers and potential customers and that its worn look does not make the impression that QRS should make. However, since the board is approving the rest of his capital budget, the president agrees to postpone the boardroom refurbishment another year. With that deletion, the capital budget is approved.

Finally, some of the directors are always concerned about conservative budgets, because of the profit-based bonuses. Some directors feel that management is overpaid without any bonus, but others want to see the officers get good bonuses. After emotional discussion, the board approves a budget that removes about half the pad that the president had inserted.

The president leaves for his Christmas vacation generally happy with the result and happy that this unsatisfying, exhausting process is over for another year. He should not be so happy.

Conclusion

The annual budgeting process provides a chance to focus on the major problems, opportunities, and plans of the company and to express the conclusions in numbers, which give reality to the objectives and strategies of the company. That chance has been missed. In each of its divisions, QRS has problems that will not go away just because they were finessed in the budget. A stockholder would wish that the problems and priorities of QRS had been recognized and addressed forthrightly. He or she has a right to expect that some of them might have even been solved.

3

Illustrating the Solution

Before delving into powerful budgeting in depth, let's pause to see what it could have accomplished in the fictitious QRS Company of Chapter 2.

The QRS Company Strategy Statement

In a good budgeting process, the QRS Company president would have issued a one-page strategy statement as a prerequisite. Summarized to its bare essentials, it would have included the following:

"QRS is, and will stay, in the instrumentation business. It will not engage in any unrelated businesses.

"Its basic strategy is and will be to pursue attractive niches within the instrumentation market.

"For the next year, QRS will concentrate on the current businesses (divisions). Assuming a favorable result of the acquisition of New, beyond next year QRS will again look for acquisitions in other attractive instrumentation niches.

"Technology appears to have forced the Mature Division into a decline that cannot be reversed. The Mature business will be run out, maximizing cash flow and return on investment and making it last as long as possible. Investment in Mature will be limited only to those things that will optimize the runout process.

"Increased profit to exceed the decline in Mature

will be pursued aggressively in the Growth and New Divisions, and QRS investment will be concentrated in these two divisions.

"Because Service is such a high return-on-investment business, an increased rate of growth will be pursued for that division, under the constraints of minimal investment and achievement of growing profit every year."

The actual strategy statement could also include actions in particular areas and responses to particular problems—recruiting, investor relations, inventory minimization, and the like—but these are not needed for the current example.

Growth Division

In Chapter 2, the division general manager (DGM) of Growth faced the budgeting problem of being considerably below a long-term 15 percent per year profit growth projection made two years previously. Unforeseen economic problems in Growth's market, increasing material prices, and the need for more indirect expense to protect the current level of sales made profit growth questionable for the next year. The DGM also believed that he had an excellent new product that could get Growth back on track within three years but that pursuing the product correctly would severely lower the next year's profit.

His response was to increase his orders budget beyond what he believed probable to justify increased indirect and development expenses. He then added half the increases in those expenses he felt he really needed. Thus the Growth DGM neither faced nor communicated his real problems to the president and the board of directors.

In contrast, a good budgeting process would start with the assumptions process, involving the QRS president and board of directors. The important outside environmental factors (OEFs) would include material prices, the economic status of the market, competitors' actions, and the training level of customers. Corresponding assumptions would address increasing material costs, the inability to raise prices because of market conditions, and the requirement for more customer support because of competitors' actions and reduced training levels in customers' organizations. From this process, the QRS president and board of directors would obtain a good understanding of the problems facing Growth, and their profit expectations would be lowered.

The Growth DGM would use gap analysis (discussed in detail in Chapter 11) to focus on his problems and recommendations. The dimension would be profit, the goal would be the earlier five-year projection, and the status quo profit for the next year would be his estimate of what could be accomplished in light of increasing material prices, more lost business because of changes in government procurement practices, and the need for increased customer support. This gap analysis would illustrate that the goal projection could not be met, and why.

The DGM would then shift to a strategic gap analysis, again with profit as the dimension but with a three-year horizon. This would give him the platform to present and explain his recommendation for proper development of the promising new product. This recommendation would also be in the context of the QRS strategy, in which Growth is one of the two divisions designated for investment and major efforts for profit growth.

Regarding other budget techniques, Growth already used good parameters, because the indirect expense and material price problems were readily identified. However, it was stated in Chapter 2 that the board of directors had a strong focus on gross margin. In a good budgeting process, the Growth DGM would mount a campaign to convince the board that contribution margin is a better parameter for his business and that flexible budgeting would let them evaluate and measure Growth better.

With this budgeting process accomplished, the QRS president and board would understand Growth's real problems and opportunities. They would be concerned that next year's profit prospects are disappointing, but that is the reality. They might retain some criticism of the Growth DGM for missing his five-year projection but should understand that this is beyond his control; the basic causes are market economic conditions and other OEFs. The Growth DGM should gain stature from the budgeting process because he has presented a specific, promising alternative to get the division moving again: the new product development.

If QRS finances and investor relations permitted, the board would probably approve the recommended aggressive new product development and the resulting lower profit for next year. This would be in line with the strategy of emphasizing the Growth Division for the future. Even if not approved—if the Growth DGM were told to cut costs and thus increase next year's profit—the decision would be made on the basis of clear understanding of problems and alternatives.

A Customer Service Manager in the Growth Division

A customer service manager in the Growth Division had the problem that her work load was steadily increasing but the whole emphasis of the Growth DGM was on containing or cutting costs. She took a "selling" approach to her problem, aggressively arguing that she needed a 20 percent increase in budgeted cost to keep up with her work load. The DGM cut her to 10 percent, which was what she wanted in the first place. However, after the QRS president cut Growth's expense budget, the customer service manager lost the entire remaining 10 percent expense growth.

In a good budgeting process, the customer service manager would use these four techniques to make her case for increased expenses:

1. Tie her requirements to the Growth OEFs of more customer support required because of competitors' actions and the lower level of training in customers' organizations.
2. Analyze her outputs in detail and express them in specific parameters, such as response time and mean time to repair.
3. Relate the effort and cost required to these outputs, properly using data, trends, and models.
4. Define and carry out one or two gap analyses aimed at increased productivity to show true responsiveness to her superior's desire for her to "work smarter" rather than just increase cost.

In doing these things, she would relate her expense budget to the work to be done, at the same time making real efforts to improve productivity. Together with the better overall Growth Division process described in the previous section, she would probably get the 10 percent budget expense increase she needs. If not, her superiors would understand the consequences of not allowing that increase. Game playing and emotions would be replaced by facts and informed judgments.

Service Division

The problem of the Service DGM in Chapter 2 began with a change in government procurement practices that made orders and sales growth more difficult, unfortunately in the face of a doubling of the Service sales force to increase the 10 percent profit growth rate of the division. The problem was made worse because the QRS president considered the Growth DGM to be a compulsive commitment meeter and therefore believed her budgets to be always overly conservative.

It is easy to identify Service's fundamental problem in terms of budgeting techniques: a significant change in a most important OEF, government procurement practices. The response has to begin with the strategic context. Service has always concentrated exclusively on federal government business, and its strategy has so stated. The Service DGM believes that this change in procurement practices makes the government market less attractive for the foreseeable future. Therefore, before the budgeting process starts, she must make a strategy presentation to the president and the board of directors. She must say that the current strategy is unattractive and that it will take her some time and considerable work to decide on a new strategy. She must also present a clear "plan for a plan" for deciding on that new strategy.

The change in government procurement practices would have been communicated naturally to top management and the board in the assumptions process (which treats important OEFs with assumptions; see Chapter 8). There would have been no argument about the importance of this OEF to Service; the only argument might have been whether the change is permanent. What the DGM advocates responds to the uncertainty: still aggressively pursuing government business while developing an alternative strategy. This is a proper response and is likely to get the support of the president and the board. They would be disappointed with the lack of results from this year's doubling of the sales force, but presidents and boards must deal with current reality and future expectations, not "what might have been." With a good budgeting process, they would be made aware of the uncertainty of the future and the uncontrollability of the OEFs. Their appropriate demand would be that their people react forcefully to uncontrollable changes, and the Service DGM would have done this.

Additionally, the QRS president would decide that he must address the Service DGM's compulsion about meeting commitments. He would force more gap analysis upon Service. He would make the Service DGM and her people deal with goals and the status quo and the concept that there is no disgrace in having gaps. The QRS president would thus lead Service toward setting higher goals for results and performance, while fostering the realization that no one can meet *all* goals established this way. Making progress on such an attitude change is yet another way that gap analysis can be valuable.

The Material Manager in the Service Division

The Service material manager was demotivated by having the in-house repair facility cut out of the budget. He had worked long and hard on this and strongly believed in it.

In a proper budgeting process, the issue would be clarified earlier in a different way. In attacking the OEFs and assumptions before and during the early stage of budgeting, management would recognize the basic strategy problem of relying on government business. As one of the Service management team, the material manager would be involved in this process. With a new strategy probably forthcoming over the next year, would the repair facility make sense? The material manager would attack his repair cost problem in light of this question.

It probably would be decided to delay the decision on the in-house facility until the new strategy is determined. Increased repair costs for next year would be duly budgeted, and the material

manager would stay involved in a dual track of strategy and corresponding repair planning.

New Division

In Chapter 2, New had three main budgeting problems. First, the
New DGM had no confidence that New could achieve the projections for the next year that he had made to support the acquisition
of New by QRS. Second, the president of QRS did not yet understand New's business very well. Third, the New DGM was irri-
tated by the large demands of the QRS financial people for supporting data to accompany the budget. So much work was
needed to understand and generate the supporting data that he
did not carry out his own budgeting process to his satisfaction.
As a result, he "punted" on his budget, submitting what he had
projected at acquisition time and hoping that he would get lucky.

In proper budgeting, the QRS president would have instituted the assumptions process for New, discussed in detail in
Chapter 8. The important factors would be (1) the involvement of
the QRS president and the chief financial officer, as well as the
New DGM and his key management team, and (2) an off-site
meeting of two or three days to start the process. The benefits
would be as follows:

1. New's important OEFs would be defined.
2. The QRS president and chief financial officer would understand New's business much better.
3. Communications in both directions would improve from
   the key people on both sides knowing and understanding
   one another better. The problem of the "unreasonable
   support data" would probably be resolved.

In the good environment thus established, the New DGM would
admit that his pre-acquisition projections were too optimistic.
(This will be confirmed by future events in any case.) By facing
the issue, he would bring himself and the QRS president together
as the two people who need to work on the same problem.

Helped by focusing on the OEFs, the best parameters, and

the problems and goals through gap analysis, the DGM could then create a game-free budget devoted to increasing New's value. He would have the president's understanding in doing this.

Using powerful budgeting for the New Division would accelerate New's integration into QRS and make the next year more fruitful. With the necessary involvement of the board of directors in the assumptions process, the directors would also get more familiar with New's business and its prospects and problems. The president would get some criticism from the board for the lower budgeted results, but better then than later when an overoptimistic budget is missed. More important, the president and the New management team would have a budget in which both believe, plus a proper process for treating future uncertainty.

The Western Region Sales Manager in the New Division

As a key manager in New as well as a remotely located one, the western region sales manager, in a good budgeting process, would attend the planning meeting with the QRS president and the New management team. She would have the opportunity to argue her ideas, expectations, and problems. She would gain a better appreciation of the problems of both New and QRS.

She would then challenge her people with a gap analysis whose dimension is orders, resulting in an orders budget somewhat higher than the initial budget she considered challenging in Chapter 2. This orders budget would probably be accepted, with recognition and appreciation.

Mature Division

In Chapter 2, Mature, a large but declining business, was told to run out its business as long and as profitably as possible, but not to invest. Mature needed to reduce expenses for the next year's budget and had problems with morale and finding new ways to do things on a reduced scale. The approach in Chapter 2 was emotional, with long, heated review meetings and compromises that did not achieve the needed downsizing. The president of

QRS added arbitrary cost cuts, and the Mature DGM was left with the problem of squeezing more cost out of a resisting division after the budget was completed.

Done properly, Mature's budgeting process would start with communication of the runout strategic context to the Mature management team. If not already in place, this should be accompanied by intelligent incentive, transfer, and severance plans and policies that would allay some of the employees' fears about the future.

Mature's budgeting challenge is intelligent, unemotional downsizing, and all the powerful budgeting techniques are applicable. The DGM must push his people to carefully define functional outputs and relate the work to those outputs. Techniques such as activity-based costing (Chapter 9) are useful to relate indirect and administrative costs to sales and organizational outputs. The DGM must insist on proper use of data, trends, and models to relate predicted costs to the outputs. Development of various models would promote objectivity and reduce emotion. (An example of a sales model for Mature is presented in Chapter 10.) As usual, gap analysis would be useful in focusing on important parameters and developing goals and plans for productivity improvements and cost reductions.

All business runout situations share two major characteristics. First, the needed downsizing must be geared toward finding better, cheaper ways to accomplish the work, rather than making arbitrary cuts. To start with, everyone is usually quite busy. Arbitrary cuts would destroy morale, which is already shaky. The solution has to be to stop doing some things, i.e., to find new, affordable ways of doing adequate work but less of it. All the budgeting techniques recommended in this book promote objective focus on outputs, best parameters, problems, and goals; therefore, they may be more valuable in a downsizing situation than in any other.

The second common characteristic of runouts is the morale problem and the associated emotional problem that all managers have in letting go of good people, particularly those whom they have known for a long time. This is the most unpleasant problem any manager has to face, but failure to let some people go when necessary can result in having to terminate a whole organization later. There is no happy solution for this problem, but two things improve the situation significantly. The first is the package of intelligent incentive, transfer, and severance practices and policies mentioned previously. The second is the evidence that budgeting analysis has been done intelligently and decisions have been made objectively, so that the cuts are rational and necessary. If these two things are done well, the person whose job has been terminated will be sad but understanding. If not done well, that person will be angry and bitter.

The planning and actions in a good budgeting process should lengthen the runout and increase its profitability and cash flow. In this case, Mature management would have clear challenges and plans, a source of considerable satisfaction in a bad situation. An important side benefit would be that the QRS management and board of directors would be impressed with the Mature management team and organization. Eventual transfer rather than termination could become more likely.

The QRS Company Budget

With all the changes in the division budgets generated by a good budgeting process, the QRS Company budget would predict less profit for next year than did the one described in Chapter 2. Growth and New Divisions would show lower profit. Service's budgeted profit would be about the same, with lower sales but also less padding in the expenses. Mature's budgeted profit actually would be a little higher than before, with progress made on intelligent cost cutting.

The difference, however, is that this budget would have been thought through, would be objectively based, and would recognize future uncertainty and the uncontrollability of OEFs. If the outside environment behaves, the sum of profit over the next three years should be greater. (If the board approves Growth's aggressive new product development plan, it knowingly reduces next year's profit in return for longer-term benefits.)

In a powerful budgeting process, approval of the budget assumptions by the board of directors in September would be a major event. In conjunction with that approval, the QRS president would have had the board hear presentations on New's business, problems, and opportunities and also on Service's need to find a new strategy and its plans for doing so.

With the education and involvement provided by this process, the board would be better attuned to the company's opportunities and problems at the December budget review, which would be shorter and more productive. The resistance of one director to the strategy of running out Mature would have been dealt with in September, so it would not encumber the review meeting. Perhaps, impressed with the good job that management had done on the budget, the board would even have approved the refurbishment of the boardroom in the capital budget!

Conclusion

Not only would this budget have a better probability of being met than the one developed in Chapter 2, chances are that the fortunes of QRS and each of the divisions would be advanced further during the coming year. Better budgeting leads to better management, which leads to better business performance. The budgeting process would have focused the attention of QRS and division management at all levels on the important problems, good solutions to those problems, and good action plans overall. It would also have pointed out the uncertain and the uncontrollable, forcing management to react to important changes in the outside world. Beyond that, this recognition would allow management to concentrate on the things that it can improve, change, control, and influence. If the incentive compensation system is tied to the budget and is realistic, the budget would also have stifled tendencies to play psychological games during budget preparation.

This budget would also make management recognize that the OEF with the greatest impact on QRS is the change in government procurement practices, which affects Service; this factor requires the questioning and probably change of an entire division strategy. Powerful budgeting would result in major QRS actions of strategic importance, including development of the new Growth product, the search for a new strategy for Service, and heightened attention and better information for pursuing New's growth.

4

Objectives of the Budgeting Process

Detailed consideration of the characteristics of good budgeting logically starts with objectives. The superficial purpose of the annual budget is to predict the results of the following year. In reality, there are a number of valid objectives of the budgeting process. The objectives of people at various organization levels are different. To illustrate, five sets of budgeting objectives are developed in this chapter: a set for a sole owner of a company, for a public company director, for a president, for a division general manager, and for a function manager.

The Sole Owner of a Company

The simplest case for developing budgeting objectives is that of a sole owner of a company. This can be an individual person or parent corporation or anything in between.

What does a sole owner want from the budgeting process? Before considering anything else, he or she wants it to be believable, reflecting the realistic prospects of the company, not the dreams of its management. It also should be internally consistent, with its different parts matching and meshing properly—the budget would not be believable if a thousand widgets were going to be shipped with none in inventory and only a hundred produced. Also, the numbers in the budget must be accurate; those who believe that this is not a problem have probably not seen very many budgets. Thus, the sole owner's first objective is a budget that *is realistic, accurate, and internally consistent.*

What does the owner want included in the budget? He or she wants a budget that predicts that the following year's operations will meet his or her financial objectives in owning that company: (1) earn an adequate return on investment, (2) accomplish that with an acceptable degree of risk, and (3) move the company toward the owner's ultimate financial objective for it. These are universal financial objectives of businesses.

Meeting these financial objectives is not always possible. If the company is recovering from past problems, or if the economy or the company's markets are poor, the owner probably cannot get all three desired results. In such cases, at worst the owner wants a budget that promises survival, at best a budget that moves the company toward those objectives. In any case, the owner wants a budget that *predicts the best results achievable, consistent with acceptable risk and the long-term health of the company.*

Next, every owner wants the company to be well managed. He or she wants good decisions made and appropriate actions taken quickly in the face of problems and surprises. A prerequisite to this is good information. The budget's role is to serve as a means for gathering and presenting information in a way that enables and facilitates good management. To use an extreme example, a budget expressing sales only in terms of market share would be of little value, because management could not know the total market sales until well after the fact. Thus, such a budget would give no guidance for daily decisions. The owner wants a budget that *contains the information most useful for management.*

But this is not all that the owner wants from a budget. The owner will not be happy with the best results achievable and good information content if they take the company in a direction he or she does not want to go. If the owner wants the company to stay in the United States, for example, he or she will not be happy if the budget shows major selling activity in Asia. If the owner wants to own a computer company, he or she will not be happy if all the development effort is going into television sets. Therefore, another desire for the budget is that it demonstrably take the company in the direction the owner wants to go. That is, the owner wants a budget that *is consistent with strategy.*

So much for the content of the budget; the owner still wants more. The owner wants management to do all the things necessary to maximize performance, and he or she wants to know quickly if it is not doing so. The budget is, by definition, both a goal-setting and a measuring device, since it is quantitative, integrative, and focused. The owner thus wants a budget that *facilitates goal setting and measurement*.

Further, the budget is the vehicle that concretely communicates the company's strategy to its management and employees. A statement in capital letters that the company will become the leader in the widget industry is meaningless if the budget contains no development or marketing money for widgets. Conversely, if the budget contains big increases in widget development and marketing, the employees will understand that that is an important strategy without hearing any strategy statement at all. Even more important, if the owner wants to expand the widget business, he or she wants the organization to spend its creativity and energy on widgets, not on something else. Thus the owner wants a budget that *communicates strategy and plans to the organization*.

The owner has one final management concern: that the planned activities of different parts of the organization be consistent and mutually supportive. If the factory plans to bring inside a function previously subcontracted, this had better be known by recruiting, facilities, purchasing, and so on, and they all need to have the work effort and required resources planned to provide the needed support. The budgeting process is the activity that makes such plans real, quantitative, and specific. Thus, finally, the owner wants a budget that *communicates operating plans across functions*.

We can now enumerate seven objectives that sum up the sole owner's needs from the budgeting process. The owner needs a budget that:

1. Is realistic, accurate, and internally consistent
2. Plans the best results achievable consistent with acceptable risk and the long-term health of the business
3. Contains the information most useful for management
4. Is consistent with strategy

5. Facilitates goal setting and measurement
6. Communicates strategy and plans to the organization
7. Communicates operating plans across functions

The Public Company Director

As representatives of the stockholders, the public company directors want generally the same things that a sole proprietor would want, but they have a few additional concerns.

First, for the sole owner the "ultimate financial objective" for the company can be anything he or she wishes it to be. (For example, the owner may wish only to make a living and not invest further in the company.) For a public company, on the other hand, that ultimate objective must be growth in value. Public company directors must be concerned that in addition to achieving good return with acceptable risk the company provide good opportunities for additional investment. This does not change the statement of the budgeting objective but changes the way in which the budget will be evaluated.

Second, the public company directors must consider what impression the predicted performance will make on the investment community and therefore on the price of the stock. Depending on the company's situation, they may have to consider the effect on disgruntled shareholders or raiders. Therefore, for company directors the sole owner's second objective must be qualified by changing it to *plans the best results achievable consistent with acceptable risk and the long-term health of the business* and *that will be interpreted positively by the investment community.*

The budgeting objectives of the public company directors are thus the same as those of a sole owner, with this one qualification.

The President

The president naturally has the same objectives as the sole proprietor or public company directors, whichever is applicable, and this is the position at which all of them take on operational meaning. However, in addition the president has two other budgeting objectives.

First, he or she wants a budget that *can be beaten*. Both the president's power and job security are usually strongly determined by his or her credibility, and protecting that credibility is important. Moreover, many companies have incentive compensation plans for at least some management personnel; these are always related to financial results in some way, and often are directly based on performance vis-à-vis the budget. The president naturally wants the biggest bonus possible; he or she also wants the biggest bonus possible for subordinates, if they earn it.

Second, the president wants a budget that *will be approved* by the board of directors. Life gets quickly miserable for the president if the board sends him or her back to redo the budget and thus takes control of the process. A complication here is that boards are made up of a number of individuals who naturally may have different views and convictions. The board may contain opposites of optimism and pessimism on the economy and on different products or businesses. Thus, a believable budget to one director may be fantasy to another; so, "a budget that will be approved" is not a trivial objective.

Another objective common to the sole owner, public company directors, and the president takes on a different meaning for the president. From the president down to all except the lowest-level manager, everyone is both a superior and a subordinate in the budgeting process—that is, both a submitter and a reviewer. The objective "a budget that facilitates goal setting and measurement" thus becomes a two-edged sword. The president and other managers want their budget to be one that can be beaten, but they want to be sure that the budget challenges their subordinates to the best possible performance and results. On the other hand, impossible budgets and goals are demotivating, and the president wants his or her people to earn decent bonuses. The duality of this objective has to be a prominent driver of the budgeting process: reconciling the desire for budgets that can be beaten with the desire to challenge the organization to its utmost.

There are thus nine objectives for the president. He or she wants a budget that:

1. Is realistic, accurate, and internally consistent
2. Plans the best results achievable consistent with acceptable risk and the long-term health of the business (*for public companies:* and that will be interpreted positively by the investment community)
3. Contains the information most useful for management
4. Is consistent with strategy
5. Facilitates goal setting and measurement
6. Communicates strategy and plans to the organization
7. Communicates operating plans across functions
8. Will be beaten
9. Will be approved

The Division General Manager

The division general manager (DGM) is preoccupied with his or her division. The DGM wants the same things that the president wants, but for the division rather than for the company. The DGM generally feels like a person building a boat on the deck of a ship. He or she is very concerned that the ship remain afloat and that it supply the material and tools he or she needs; other than that, the DGM wishes that the ship's crew would leave him or her alone. Since the DGM is competing with other division general managers building other boats on the ship's deck, there is a new budgeting objective: a budget that *gives the division the largest possible portion of the company's resources.*

Another concern about the company is that it reassure the DGM that it is going in a good direction. In this regard, for all participants below the president, a statement must be added to the president's fourth objective: *and that reassures him or her that the company is moving in a good direction.* All employees need to feel good about what the company is doing and its prospects; lower-level employees need the same feeling about their divisions and particular departments. Management needs to continually communicate this confidence, and all managers need to feel it themselves. No one wants to work for a company that he or she feels is doing the wrong things.

Otherwise, the DGM's budgeting objectives are similar to the president's, but generally applied to the division. The DGM wants a budget that:

1. Is realistic, accurate, and internally consistent
2. Plans the best results achievable for the division, consistent with acceptable risk and the long-term health of the division
3. Contains the information most useful for management
4. Is consistent with the division's strategy, plus a company budget that reassures him or her that the company is moving in a good direction
5. Facilitates goal setting and measurement within the division
6. Communicates division strategy and plans to the division organization and to other divisions
7. Communicates operating plans across functions within the division
8. Will be beaten
9. Will be approved
10. Gives the division the largest possible portion of the company's resources

The Functional Manager

The functional manager, any manager who does not have profit and loss responsibility, is concerned about the total company. However, this concern is only an indirect, "reassure me" type of concern. The functional manager's primary concern is, and should be, his or her particular function. To do the job, a functional manager needs to know what is expected, what resources are available, how to interface with other elements of the organization, and what support will be received from them. Different functions are strongly interdependent, and their work and planning must be closely coordinated. Since the budget is the quantitative vehicle for expressing these needs, these concerns become their primary budgeting objectives.

In addition to these different primary objectives, the functional manager shares some budgeting objectives with the division general manager. The functional manager also wants a realistic budget that contains the most useful information, wants the largest possible portion of company resources, and so forth. The functional manager needs to know the company and division strategies, because his or her budget must be consistent with them. The functional manager, then, wants a budget that:

1. Is realistic, accurate, and internally consistent
2. Tells what he or she is expected to accomplish (the outputs)
3. Contains the information most useful for management
4. Communicates strategy and reassures the functional manager that the company and the division are moving in a good direction
5. Facilitates goal setting and measurement for the functional manager and subordinates
6. Gives the functional manager the needed resources
7. Gives the functional manager the needed support from other functions
8. Will be beaten
9. Will be approved
10. Gives the function the largest possible portion of company resources

Conclusion: Good News and Bad News

The foregoing examples are broad enough to illustrate the different objectives of all the participants in the budgeting process. To be successful, the process must be responsive to the needs of *all* of them.

The good news is that, while differing in object and application, these objectives are similar enough that a sufficiently realistic composite set of objectives can be presented. Such a composite set can validly meld the objectives of all participants, with the understanding that the concern and focus will differ among them, and is used in Chapter 6 as one of the bases for "Requirements for a Powerful Budgeting Process."

This composite set of budgeting objectives is a budget that:

1. Is realistic, accurate, and internally consistent
2. Plans the best results achievable for the company and its divisions consistent with acceptable risk and the long-term health of the business (and that will be interpreted positively by the investment community)
3. Contains the information most useful for management
4. Is consistent with a strategy that reassures employees that the company is moving in a good direction
5. Facilitates goal setting and measurement at all levels
6. Communicates strategy, plans, and required outputs to the organization
7. Communicates operating plans, including support needs, across functions
8. Will be beaten
9. Will be approved
10. Gives every department the resources it needs to meet its budget

The bad news is that there is a significant conflict within the budgeting objectives*: the contradiction between planning "the best results achievable" and a budget that "will be beaten." Every participant from the president down has this fundamental conflict. Management owes its owner(s) the best results achievable under given conditions. However, every level of management needs to reinforce its credibility and will always have a strong drive to get a budget approved that can be beaten.

This conflict of objectives is the first of the inherent budgeting problems. It is fundamental to the activity of budgeting and can-

---

*There is another conflict among the objectives of all the participants below the president. Each wants the "largest possible portion of corporate resources" to be put at his or her disposal. This is not considered here as a *budgeting* conflict, however, because this is normal organizational conflict, basic to business management. Any executive wants advocacy from subordinates; the stronger and more intelligent the advocacy, the better the decisions he or she can make regarding alternative actions and allocation of resources. This conflict will not be further considered here, except to note that a good budgeting process will provide the information needed to decide such alternatives and allocations.

not be avoided or removed. A budgeting process must be designed to meet the objectives while minimizing the adverse effects of the inherent problems, yielding the best possible planning document. In Chapter 5 the other inherent problems of budgeting are identified and discussed.

5

Inherent Problems to Overcome

Problems inherent in budgeting cause typical irrationalities and game playing, even among the best and brightest people. The conflict of objectives among the participants, discussed in Chapter 4, is the first of these inherent problems. Another is that managers are measured on performance vis-à-vis the budget. A third problem exists because the budget fundamentally deals with uncertainty—i.e., the future. Fourth, major factors that affect a business are beyond its control. The final inherent problem is that budgeting is fundamentally an exercise in psychology, rather than logic or arithmetic. All these problems are related and reinforce one another.

Measurement

Measuring and rewarding management on the basis of financial results is so obviously appropriate that it is impossible to conceive of not doing it. There are good arguments for tying bonuses to actual performance versus budget. However, it must be clearly understood that measurement is the enemy of realistic budgeting.

Because compensation and even job security are involved, managers do not plan the best results achievable; they are as conservative as the approval process allows. Their budgets contain hidden pads and pockets of contingency funds. Further, budgets that could be beaten may not be. Managers ensure that all budgeted money is spent, both so that they will not be accused of submitting an unrealistic budget and so that their funds will not be cut in the following year.* (This is a familiar phenomenon in government; there is often a spate of year-end procurements to spend leftover funds.) Also, managers tend to relax if they see that their budget will be easily met. Instead of pushing well beyond budgeted performance, and thereby opening themselves to the possibility of having submitted unrealistic budgets, they add expenses for a perceived longer-term benefit or something that will reduce their personal risk.

There is an even more fundamental problem related to measurement: Business management is inherently difficult to measure. This is heretical by today's standards of incessant criticism and frequent replacement of management, so elaboration is in order.

Every manager who has been in a job for more than a few years believes that in some years he or she made great contributions and in some years little real contribution, and that *his or her financial results, and probably bonus, are essentially uncorrelated with those contributions*. In some situations, breaking even is super performance; in some situations, achieving the budget is bad performance. And such situations can change very rapidly.

One school of thought says that managers are paid to overcome problems and there is no valid excuse for not meeting commitments, including budgets. This is not always true. To take two well-known examples, consider the airline industry after the oil shocks in the 1970s and the aerospace industry after the cold war suddenly ended in 1989. Both of these events were sudden and totally unpredicted. There is no way that airline or aerospace companies could have met budgets developed before those sudden

*Another problem of measurement against budget is that it leads to irrational actions at year-end. Everyone in industry has seen companies offer special discounts if the order is placed before year-end. Also, many factories pay overtime and even holiday premium pay to maximize shipments before year-end. Such actions are motivated by the desire to maximize reported results for investor relations and measurement/bonus purposes. To step back a little, however, carrying this to extremes of special discounts, holiday pay, and the like is ridiculous. In the long run, it makes little difference if an item is shipped on December 31 rather than January 6; spending considerable money to accomplish shipment on December 31 makes little sense. But such practices will continue as long as public companies report on an annual basis and the measurement implications of inflexible budgets are strong.

events; there was nothing management could do in the short term to overcome them.

Countless smaller but decisive events happen every day to all businesses. In every business there is a range of important uncertainties that the managers are supposed to manage. However, they will be powerless in the short term against the large, unpredictable changes that happen. For example, if a company has a major customer that accounts for an appreciable percentage of total sales, any management should be expected to accommodate reasonable variations in sales to that customer. However, if that major customer suddenly and surprisingly cancels its business, no management could be expected to immediately fill that hole in sales. Further, management would have been properly criticized if it had budgeted no sales from this major customer. Planning for such an improbable event would have taken away the resources to fill the probable orders. If that major customer suddenly disappears, management may well do the best job it has ever done—if it cuts expenses intelligently but increases marketing and sales and the company can be seen to be well on its way to filling the hole in sales in one or two years—even while badly missing its budget for that year.

The best management jobs are sometimes accomplished in bad years, and management should not be punished unthinkingly just because of a bad year or because the stock price goes down. Luck plays a larger part in business results than most people are willing to admit. And surprises, totally unpredictable at the time, happen every day. In fact, this is so large a factor in present-day business that in an ideal world, the primary measurement of management would not be the year-end numbers, but rather the quality of management's reaction to surprises.

Uncertain Future

Another inherent problem is the uncertainty of the future. The only certainty that anyone can count on is that things will change and there will be surprises. Dealing with the future is what managers get paid for doing. There is never complete information on which to base decisions; managers deal with uncertainty by using the best information available, hedging their bets, and allowing for contingencies. Good managers do not make "bet the company" decisions unless circumstances force them to do so. The uncertainty of the future is not news to any manager.

Budgets, however, by their numerical and detailed nature, imply and demand specificity. A manager is not asked for a range of probable sales for next year; he or she is asked for a single number. Ranges for each sales and expense category would give such a wide range for total sales, expense, and profit as to be meaningless.

The effect of an uncertain future can be either optimism or pessimism, depending on the participant. The cautious type will pad the budget, promising poorer results than really expected. The optimistic type will have unreasonable faith in the future and promise the moon. In any case, the budget will be less probable than its specificity implies. And if the uncertainty is not deliberately considered, it will later be difficult to decide whether good or bad results are primarily because of performance or luck.

The Environment Will Not Hold Still

A main cause of uncertainty about the future is that the relevant environment is not static. By *environment* is meant all the things outside a company that influence its business. While the specific environmental elements and their relative importance are different for every company, they can be generalized into five groups: market, industry, economy, government, and financial.

The *market* environment includes all customer needs and preferences and the continuous changes therein. One company's market may be all the doctors in one American county, while another company's market may be all the consumers in one hundred countries throughout the world. Whatever the relevant market, both its influence on a company and its uncontrollable nature are obvious.

The *industry* environment refers to the industry in which the company is situated. It includes both overall industry changes that will enlarge or diminish industry profit and actions by competitors who attempt to rearrange market share and profits within the industry. The calculator industry offers a good example of this environment. About twenty years ago technological advances in electronics led to the demise of a large industry that supplied mechanical calculators and at the same time gave rise to a large industry that supplied electronic calculators. Then the electronic calculators changed so quickly in cost and features that competitive actions led to the rise and fall of entire companies in a matter of a few years. Unfortunately for the cause of stable budgets, competitors and even whole industries can rise and fall rather abruptly.

The *economy* as an environment refers to all the wealth and monetary factors outside a particular market or industry. They tend to affect all business, but, of course, not uniformly. The obvious elements are booms and recessions, which raise or lower the sales levels of most businesses. Particular items, either localized or global, can be more important, however. Global economic events that affected most businesses were the oil shocks of the 1970s: Almost every business experienced immediate cost increases. An example of a localized event is the effect of closing a military base on all consumer-oriented businesses in the surrounding area.

The *government* category includes all things that all governments do that are relevant to the business. There are many government laws and regulations on many subjects, and the number of both regulations and subjects covered always seems to increase. Environmental laws hardly existed twenty years ago, yet their effects have already bankrupted some businesses and become a major financial concern for others. In addition to laws and regulations, a wide variety of government decisions can affect a company. Again as examples both global and local, a decision by the federal government banning trade with a particular country would have major effects on a number of companies, while a decision of a town to contract out its garbage collection could have a major effect on a few companies.

The *financial* environment includes changes in banking policies, stockholder actions and perceptions, and the investment/financial community in general. They are grouped into one category because the fundamental effect of all of them on a business is their influence on how and whether the business can get the money it needs. Credit can be loose or tight, and it can be easy, difficult, or impossible to sell new stock at any given time independently of what the company is doing. This category also includes the potentially large effect of attitudes, particularly in troublesome times. The degree of hostility by particular shareholders (possibly leading to lawsuits or proxy fights), whether a bank will agree to temporary waivers on loan covenants, and so on are important for a business and possibly totally out of the company's control. In the short term, no public company has a choice in the matter of whether a raider targets it for takeover.

The nature of each company determines the specific make-up of the pertinent outside environments and also the relative importance of the various factors. The pertinent points for the budgeting process are that (1) these outside environments are very important in determining the next year's results, (2) they generally exhibit ever-accelerating change, (3) the only thing certain about them is that some of them *will* change significantly during the next year, and, therefore, (4) their change is an inherent problem in budgeting realistically. In fact, these environments are often more important than management in determining the results of a business. Bad management can cause failure in a good environment, but good management usually cannot overcome bad outside environments in the short term. (In the long term, presumably, good management will take steps to get the company out of the bad environments.)

All budgets are based on assumptions, either implicit or explicit, about the pertinent environments. In retrospect, the smaller environmental changes that affected results were predictable; if they were not factored into the budget, that was a problem with the budgeting process. On the other hand, the "super-changes," which can have the largest effects, often come as complete surprises. *Nobody* predicted the breakdown of the Soviet Union, which culminated in its dissolution in 1991.

Psychology

Budgeting is essentially a psychological process. This follows unavoidably from the conflict in objectives in which the superior wants the best results possible and the organization to be challenged, while the subordinate wants a budget he or she can beat. It also follows from the uncertainty with which both superior and subordinate are dealing; neither knows what the future will hold, or even exactly what resources will be needed to do a specified job. With these contradictory objectives plus the uncertainty, both superior and subordinate go through a mental process of guessing the other's state of mind.

In preparing budget numbers, the smart subordinate first gets the best picture possible of what the next year will bring and what resources will be needed. (This involves the same psychological exercise with *his* or *her* subordinates, of course.) After that, the first question is, "How will the boss react to this?" He or she then thinks about the boss's attitude generally, reaction to past budgets, what he or she has said and done lately, and current pressures. The subordinate also judges how smart the boss is, where he or she can be fooled, and where the subordinate had better not try to fool the boss. The distillation of all such thinking determines the transition from what the subordinate thinks is a realistic budget to the budget actually submitted to the superior.

A simple but trivial example is the case in which the subordinate knows that the superior has arbitrarily cut everybody's submitted expenses every year by 5 percent. It does not take a Rhodes scholar to figure out that this subordinate should pad expenses beyond what he or she thinks is needed. The usual psychological games are more sophisticated and complex; few superiors are that simple and predictable. (I have watched and experienced, however, the consternation when the superior reacts to submitted budgets in a totally different and unpredicted way. I would recommend this once in a while to all bosses; this is one area in which the organization benefits if the boss is not predictable.) Some subordinates are naturally better at this game than others; it is painful to watch a totally straightforward person try to be devious.

Now it is the superior's turn. If he or she is good, the boss is both compassionate and suspicious at budget time, as well as being competent and conscientious, which he or she should always be. Compassion makes the boss want the subordinate to get a fair budget that can be met and possibly beaten, but not by too much. The suspicious boss is skeptical of every number the subordinate presents. The first question the superior asks is, "Is this person an optimist or a pessimist?" The second (and more important) question is, "What is this person's record in meeting commitments? Can I count on him to perform as promised?" Then the boss considers the current pressures on the subordinate, known positions on various decisions and directions, the extent of knowledge in various areas, and general intelligence. The boss also considers whether the subordinate is a polished game player or not. The boss ordinarily has a preconceived idea of approximately what the subordinate's budget should be, and this is usually modified somewhat by good subordinate input during the budgeting process. The superior uses all these questions and thought processes to convert the submitted budget to one with which he or she is comfortable.

The superior has the advantage over the subordinate in this psychological game. The boss is in the controlling position and is reacting rather than initiating. A good boss goes as far as he or she can objectively, and a good boss will be both smart and knowledgeable of the subordinate's work. However, unless the organization is weak, the subordinate will know more about his or her work than the superior knows. In any event, both are dealing with the uncertain future. Therefore, objective inquiry only takes one so far. The superior then resorts to psychology to finally get to the budget that *he* or *she* thinks is proper.

The straightforward way to modify a subordinate's budget is to analyze it logically, line by line if necessary. While logical analysis is proper in any budget review, it is not always the best way to handle the process. If the subordinate's budget is far off what the superior wants and thinks is possible, the completely arbitrary approach of literally throwing it at the subordinate, with the admonition, "This is nonsense—come back with a budget that is worth my time!" can be highly effective. No discussion, no explanation. This is like a service ace in the budgeting game—there is no defense and, illogically, it can yield a marked improvement without any other effort by the superior.

You may be asking, "If you have all this game playing, why not get better people rather than put up with such nonsense?" It is not that the people involved are bad or devious. The game playing is an inherent problem in the budgeting process, due in this case to a conflict in objectives and uncertainty about the future. You may also be thinking, "All these high-priced and smart people are supposed to reason together to the best result, and be objective." No, every organization has built-in conflicts and adversarial situations, and these are fundamental to successful operation. "Objective" is in the eye of the beholder; a good boss wants his or her people to be advocates, not passive people who agree to everything.

Superior and subordinate eventually arrive at an agreed budget, with which each has different degrees of comfort. (As in any negotiation, the result is probably better if both sides have about an equal degree of discomfort.) The problem is that the psychology can easily overwhelm the reality, so that the latter is never fully addressed. The final budget becomes far less than the optimum one sought.

This psychological game is ordinarily what makes the budgeting process so painful. Budget reviews can get very emotional—and long. There can be considerable anguish on both sides as the subordinate ponders what to do to make the boss understand his or her needs, and the superior ponders how to get the subordinate committed to a budget the boss thinks is proper. No one enjoys the process, except possibly a sadistic budget analyst who enjoys seeing the executives under stress.

There is a particular budgeting phenomenon that is inexplicable except in these psychological terms. All the discussion here has been about the motivation of the subordinate to get the most comfortable possible budget approved. In the face of this logic, most managers have encountered the wildly optimistic budgeter: one who predicts and promises results far beyond what the superior expects and needs. This employee volunteers to leap tall buildings at a single bound, even when the boss believes the person cannot do it and, furthermore, is happy for him or her to walk around the buildings. Unless the person in question is a salesperson (as someone once said, "If a salesman is not an optimist, he is nothing"), the superior will worry about his or her maturity. The only explanation for this budgeting behavior must be psychological: perhaps it is the desire for approval, the feeling that a high expense level is needed that can only be justified by the optimistic results, the postponement of a confrontation in the hope it will go away, or some other such reason. A superior quickly learns who the optimists are. The consolation is that the reviews are easier, since the boss reduces the results rather than exhorting improvement, but the problem is that the boss will have a difficult time learning what is realistic.

Conclusion: The Budgeting Problem

It should now be apparent why it is so difficult to generate good budgets. The budget deals with the future, and many things about the future are uncertain and uncontrollable. Further, the people most knowledgeable about the business, the functional managers directly on the firing line, are not motivated to be realistic in their budget submissions. The finished budget is then (usually) cast in concrete and (always) used to measure the participants.

These facts would lead to game playing by the best and the brightest. Unfortunately, few companies are populated exclusively with the best and the brightest, and all imperfections exacerbate the problems. The usual result is a painful process that generates a document of limited usefulness, instead of the potentially most useful planning tool possible.

The inherent problems will not go away; they are fundamental to any budgeting situation. However, they can and must be surmounted for the budget to be a useful planning document. The techniques and process for accomplishing this are the subject of Part II.

6

Requirements for a Powerful Budgeting Process

What kind of budgeting process is needed to realize the potential of the budget as the company's most powerful planning document? Clearly, a process focused on attaining the budgeting objectives while minimizing the effects of the inherent problems.

From Chapter 4, the ten composite budgeting objectives define a budget that:

1. Is realistic, accurate, and internally consistent
2. Plans the best results achievable for the company and its divisions consistent with acceptable risk and long-term health (and that will be interpreted positively by the investment community)
3. Contains the information most useful for management
4. Is consistent with a strategy that reassures employees that the company is moving in a good direction
5. Facilitates goal setting and measurement at all levels
6. Communicates strategy, plans, and required outputs to the organization
7. Communicates operating plans, including support needs, across functions
8. Will be beaten
9. Will be approved
10. Gives every organization the resources it needs to meet its budgets

From Chapter 5, five inherent problems of budgeting must be overcome:

1. The conflict at various levels between the objectives "the best results achievable" and "a budget that will be beaten"
2. The negative effect of measurement upon realistic budgeting
3. The uncertainty of the future
4. The uncontrollability of important outside environmental factors
5. The essentially psychological nature of budgeting

Overcoming Inherent Problems

It is well to consider the inherent problems first, because, as said previously, they will never go away. The future will always hold uncertainty, and the necessity of measurement in budgeting will always promote conservatism. The appropriate goal for the budgeting process is to address these problems deliberately in a way that will neutralize their negative effects.

These negative effects make the budget more emotionally based and cause people to predict lower performance than is possible. They also make the participants concerned more with getting their budgets approved than with striving for the best performance and the best solutions to the company's problems. The result is generally a budget that is less meaningful than it could be, one that is not a powerful management tool. The conflict of objectives, the negative effect of measurement, and the psychological nature of budgeting contribute directly to this problem. The uncertainty of the future and the uncontrollability of external factors make the problem worse by worrying the budgeting participants into being even more conservative.

The keys to overcoming these inherent problems are to focus the attention of all budgeting participants on what the company wants to do, on its real problems and opportunities, and on continual striving for improvement and excellence. The requirements are to:

1. Ensure that everything in the budgeting process promotes objectivity and concentration on the real strategy, opportunities, and problems of the company.
2. Deal realistically with uncertainty and uncontrollability, so that these are removed as a cause of confusion and as an excuse for lower budgets. They also need to be removed as a later excuse for missing the budget.
3. Focus the organization's attention on the parameters most important to company performance and strategy and demand the best possible numerical predictions for all parameters.
4. Include a deliberate mechanism for promoting improvement and encouraging excellence throughout the company.

Meeting Objectives

The budgeting requirements that flow from a company's objectives can be determined by discussing the first five composite objectives mentioned at the beginning of this chapter.

What is needed to promote a "realistic, accurate, and internally consistent" budget? On a conceptual level, this requires that the budget emphasize and promote the right things, i.e., that it be developed in the proper strategic context. Also, it must deal realistically with the uncertain future and with uncontrollable external factors. At the implementation level, the focus must be on the right parameters, and the budget must display the best possible numerical predictions of the future. Finally, on the mechanical level, the process flow must be designed to include appropriate checking and review and must make proper use of modern information technology.

To achieve a budget that "plans the best results achievable . . . ," the primary requirement is to have a deliberate mechanism for promoting continuous improvement and encouraging excellence. This is probably the most difficult objective to meet, because all the inherent problems are arrayed against it; they all conspire to make people naturally budget lower performance than is possible. Once the figures are "set in concrete" by approval of the budget, managers often aim no higher than meeting this conservative budget. A mechanism that promotes continuous improvement and excellent performance may ultimately be the key to the company's survival.

To produce a budget that meets the third composite objective, "contains the information most useful to management," management must have the information that facilitates the best decisions and actions. This means focusing on the most meaningful parameters and developing the most intelligent prediction of numerical results. For information to be most useful to management, the budget must also be consistent with strategy and deal realistically with the uncertain and uncontrollable.

The fourth objective, a budget that is "consistent with strategy," requires two things: that the budget be prepared in a proper strategic context and that the flow of the budgeting process be designed in a way to keep the strategy firmly implanted in the budget.

To "facilitate goal setting and measurement" through budgeting, the fifth objective, clear emphasis must be placed on the most important things that management can control and influence. This in turn requires that the budget be prepared in the proper strategic context, that it deal realistically with the uncertain and uncontrollable, and that it focus on the most important parameters.

The other five objectives are concerned with communication, meeting the budget, budget approval, and proper allocation of resources. If it is emphasized that the process flow must ensure proper communication and involvement up and down the organization and provide the basis for timely decisions, the already stated requirements will satisfy these objectives, too.

In sum, the requirements of a good budgeting process are these:

1. The budget must be prepared in the proper strategic context, firmly within the framework of the objectives, strategies, and plans of the company.
2. The process must deal realistically with uncertainty and uncontrollability.

3. A budget format that provides the most useful information for management must be used.
4. The content must provide the best possible numerical predictions of next year's results.
5. The process must emphasize encouragement of excellence at all levels within the company.
6. A coherent, efficient, and timely process flow must tie everything together.

If these requirements can be met, the budget will fulfill its potential as the company's most useful planning document and make the budgeting process a powerful contributor to better business performance.

Implementing the Budgeting Process

Processes and techniques to meet these six budgeting requirements are the subject of Part II.

Chapter 7 treats the placement of the budgeting process in the proper strategic context.

Chapter 8 presents the assumptions process, which is one of the best ways to deal with uncertainty and uncontrollability, because it directly treats the important OEFs. In the discussion of the assumptions process, the argument for willingness to change the budget is developed, and a superior role for the board of directors in company affairs is advocated.

The subject of Chapter 9 is budget format, covering ways to make the budget most useful to management. The chapter explains how to focus on the parameters that best portray the benefits and consequences of management actions.

Chapter 10 covers budget content and the correct use of the three sources of budget numbers: data, trends, and models.

Chapter 11 addresses the problem of encouraging excellence through the process of gap analysis. In addition to being a most useful tool for encouraging excellence, gap analysis confers many benefits in problem solving and communication, both up and down the organization and across functions.

Chapter 12 puts it all together with the presentation of a coherent, effective, and efficient process flow. The problems in changing from routine budgeting procedures to a powerful budgeting process are discussed at the end of Chapter 12.

FUNCTIONAL MANAGERS: SURMOUNTING A POOR BUDGETING PROCESS

What about functional managers whose company's budgeting process does not meet the above requirements? As discussed in the Introduction, they can do quite a bit: improve their own budgets, encourage their superiors and neighbor departments to adopt better budgets, and perhaps even promote improved budgeting for their division or company. Use of the recommended budgeting process and techniques by functional managers is discussed at the ends of Chapters 7 through 12.

Should the Functional Manager Try to Change the Budgeting Process?

When the performance of a functional manager's company would improve if the company adopted the budgeting process recommended in this book and the functional manager could make a significant contribution by spearheading the drive to powerful budgeting. Should he or she start a campaign to change the company's budgeting process?

The best general advice is this: The *smartest* thing that an ambitious manager can do is to jump into a pit full of tigers *if* his or her superiors know that the tigers are there *and* are interested in the pit. The *dumbest* thing that an ambitious manager can do is to jump into a pit full of tigers either if the superiors do not think any tigers are there or if they are not interested in that particular pit. Examples abound of reputations made by individuals tackling and fixing products, programs, and divisions that were in crisis. Not as publicized are managers who took over crisis organizations in which the crisis was not recognized; such managers generally fail—and get the blame for the failure.

Applying this advice to budgeting: If the company's management is truly fed up with the budgeting process *and* believes that it is important, *and* believes that getting an adequate budgeting process will require major effort, it will welcome anyone who comes forward with ideas to improve it. In that case, management is interested in the pit and knows about the tigers.

However, if company management is preoccupied with other problems it considers more important, the worst thing one could do is to start agitating for a major budgeting improvement program. The best management in the world would have no patience for a budgeting presentation if the company's biggest customer had just canceled or the entire sales force had just resigned to join a competitor.

Additionally, the reputation of the advocating functional manager is important. If the person has earned a reputation for competence and accomplishment, management will be predisposed to listen. If he or she has been a frequent agitator for half-baked proposals, management will not pay much attention to even an excellent proposition.

Finally, the position and attitude of accounting is important. The design and maintenance of the budgeting process is often the responsibility of accounting. Unenlightened controllers and accounting managers emphasize the part of their responsibility that calls for protecting the company's assets and properly reporting financial results and deemphasize their responsibility to provide the financial information management needs to run the business. This can be a "rice bowl" issue, with such accounting people fighting against any functional manager who tries to invade what they see as *their* turf. If accounting is thus unenlightened and strong in the company, the functional manager will be hard put to change the company budgeting process.

Thus, a functional manager should undertake an initiative to foster major improvements in the company's budgeting process *if and only if* (1) management is demonstrably unhappy with current budgeting, (2) management believes in the importance of good budgeting, (3) the functional manager has the reputation and prestige that will cause peers and superiors to follow his or her leadership, and (4) accounting will not ardently fight the change. If all four conditions are met, the functional manager should volunteer to head a task force whose goal is better budgeting for the company or division. By so doing, he or she will make, and be recognized for, a major contribution.

If all four conditions are not met, the functional manager should settle for more modest goals: to improve his or her own budgeting, to influence superiors and departments with which he or she interacts to adopt better budgeting, and to work to garner more widespread interest in the subject when demonstrated improvements result from these modest efforts.

Influencing Neighbor Departments

The work of different functions is so intertwined that the effects of good budgeting increase significantly as good practices broaden. There are only two ways to influence superiors and other managers in associated departments: example and persuasion. Generally, example should precede persuasion. At the beginning of the quest for better budgeting, the functional manager should work quietly until he or she has demonstrated good results.

Then he or she can start the persuasion from a position of accomplishment. The only exception is gap analysis, which can and should be advocated at any time as a useful approach to multifunction problem solving.

The sequence and pace of the persuasion depend on the culture of the organization and the management styles and personalities involved. A good starting point ordinarily is to convince a peer department to supply new or different inputs to the functional manager's budgeting. Another good early action is to solicit the help of the superior and peer managers in defining the outside environmental factors (OEFs), the internal uncontrollable factors (IUFs; see Chapter 8), and the assumptions for his or her function. As others get involved and begin to understand and see the benefits of what the functional manager is doing, the functional manager can start advocating good practices for the superior's whole organization, and in peer departments.

Be careful in advocating different budget formats for related departments. Unless it is clearly understood as limited, supplementary information, the functional manager's private format will then no longer be private. This can raise the "rice bowl" issue with accounting and possibly look like a form of mutiny to top management. The best way to change budget format outside one's own function is to persuade accounting and management that the change should be made officially.

A good time to advocate improved budgeting is when major changes in output or major cost reductions must be made. Such major changes always pose difficulties for managers and should make them receptive to a fresh approach. For example, a business acquisition may increase and broaden the work load of human resources. At that time, the vice-president of human resources may welcome the advocacy by his recruiting manager of a new approach to budgeting that promises to improve planning and problem solving.

A functional manager can surmount a poor budgeting process and thereby achieve better performance and greater job satisfaction. If conditions are right, he or she can make a major contribution to the company by spearheading an improvement in company budgeting. If conditions are not right for that, functional managers can still improve their own budgets. Further, the functional manager can increase the benefits of better budgeting across associated departments. If the functional manager does this, he or she will not get nearly as many scratches from the many tigers that *he* or *she* knows are in the pit.

Part II
Satisfying
the Requirements

7

Establishing the Context: Strategy, Plan, Budget

Making the budget consistent with the strategic plan seems an obvious requirement. Yet it is often not done. Some companies have no explicit strategy, so making the budget consistent with strategy is guesswork on the part of participants below the president. Other companies have what they call strategic plans, but these are not really operative in the management of the business. And there is often a curious barrier between strategic planning and budgeting; it sometimes seems that the strategic plans and budgets were prepared in different worlds.

The fundamental problem is again psychological: The motivations of the participants in strategic planning and budgeting are quite different. Consider a division general manager, or a product or marketing manager. If the strategic plan emphasizes long-term projections, as it often does, these managers are motivated to make their divisions or products appealing. Their personal goals are to get company attention and resources committed to their "babies." Therefore, long-range projections tend to be overoptimistic. On the other hand, in budgeting, managers are motivated to submit the least challenging budget they can get approved; they emphasize the difficulties and problems their products or divisions face. The result is that a submitted budget can be surprisingly worse than the comparable projections in the strategic plan.

A good budgeting process should embed the budget within the strategy and plans. The first necessary step is to have a meaningful, well-communicated strategy.

Strategic Planning

Strategic planning is a major subject in management theory and practice. Its application and even its definition are controversial, and different approaches ebb and flow in popularity. Detailed treatment of the subject is beyond the scope of this book, but here are some general comments on strategic planning:

1. *Every company has a strategy.* One may have a two-inch-thick strategic plan while in another the strategy exists only in the mind of the owner or the president. In the worst case the strategy may change every month. But it is impossible not to have a strategy, meaning a body of thought that sets and guides the company's goals and actions.

2. *Top management cannot delegate strategic planning.* For a stated strategy or strategic plan to have meaning, it must reflect the convictions and preferences of the top executive. There is almost always a choice of strategies available; the one chosen must reflect the direction in which the top executive wants to take the company. Without his or her direct involvement, the strategic plan is just an interesting, or onerous, exercise.

3. *The process should be outside-in.* It should begin with the outside environmental factors (OEFs) that have significant influence on the business. These OEFs define the pertinent parameters within which the company will operate. The capabilities and planned actions should be fit to the outside world rather than vice versa.

4. *The most important strategic decision a company makes is the concentration decision* — where it will focus its efforts and resources. Also important and implicit in the decision is its converse — the areas on which the company will *not* focus. It should be possible to state a company's strategy on one piece of paper, and this should be done. (An example of a one-page strategy statement is given in Chapter 3 for the fictitious QRS Company.) The rest of a strategic plan should be justification for it plus delineation of the actions needed to carry out the strategy, along with plans for implementing those actions.

5. *Financial projections should be minimized.* The importance of

a strategic plan is the decision on how the company will position itself in the marketplace, not on financial predictions for the long-term future. The purpose of strategic planning is to determine how the company will address that future.

There is a large body of theory and techniques available on the subject of strategic planning; any technique that yields the above results is suitable.

Establishing Proper Context

In addition to the different budgeting motivations of the partici-pants, there are often a number of other difficulties in embedding the budget in the strategy.

The first occurs in a situation in which there is no explicitly communicated strategy. In this case, budgeting participants have to guess, resulting in a bottom-up budget that tends to look like a budget developed by a committee, with contradictions and incon-sistencies. There are many good reasons for developing and pub-lishing a strategy, but the pain of budgeting with no strategic con-text is reason enough by itself.

Similarly, if a strategic plan has been prepared without mean-ingful top-management involvement, this lack will be discovered at budget time. The lower levels will submit budgets they think are in the proper strategic context and be surprised and confused when attacked for proposing the wrong emphasis. For example, the strategic plan may say that concentration will be on products A and B for future growth, and then the president cuts related marketing expenses. The results are (1) a realization at all levels that the strategic plan did not mean much (and skepticism the next time the troops are asked to work hard on a new strategic plan) and (2) a chaotic budgeting process.

Unfortunately, I have seen the same type of situation when the president was strongly involved in strategic planning. I have heard a president, in presenting his strategic plan, emphasize cer-tain products with high hopes and radiate optimism about the future; six months later he was cutting budgets to the bone while talking of nothing but severe short-term problems. This illustrates the next problem: Amazingly, strategic plans sometimes seem to be prepared in a different world from budgets. (It seems that somehow a part of the brain turns off during strategic planning, and an opposite part turns off during budgeting.) The result can be an impressive-looking strategic plan that is not meaningful because its essential implementation in the budget is missing. The only possible explanation is that strategic planning is not taken seriously; it is done primarily because "every good company does strategic planning," and there is little measurement connotation associated with it. Budgets, on the other hand, are serious things that will be used every day to manage the company and measure the managers.

The final problem regarding embedding the budget in a strategic context arises when the strategic plan emphasizes detailed numbers in long-range financial projections. This tends to insert all the budgeting problems noted in Part I into the strategic planning process. Such emphasis makes the strategy process degenerate into number crunching, leaving insufficient time and energy to generate the one-page strategy statement.

Top-Down vs. Bottom-Up Budgeting

Exclusive reliance on either top-down or bottom-up budgeting usually produces poor results. If the budget is totally bottom-up, results are inconsistent and contradictory. All managers submit what they think they need, balanced by what they believe top management wants. In the absence of direction or guidance from top management, the perception of "what top management wants" naturally varies from participant to participant. On the other hand, a budget that is totally top-down, meaning that top management dictates the results of the budgeting process, carries with it no commitment by the organization. It is always "his budget" or "her budget," rather than "my budget."

The solution, of course, is to include elements of both. The expectations of top management should be known, but the inputs of what can be sold, what can be done, and how much things will cost should be made by the people with the best information. These are the people closest to the problems, i.e., the functional managers and their key people. The best approach, then, is one in which the direction and guidance of top management is communicated in a way that does not intrude on the process of getting specific inputs from the most knowledgeable and qualified people. Top management communicates the "why" and the "what" in overall terms, while the lower levels provide the "what" in detail, the "how," and the "how much."

The strategy/plans context is an excellent way for top management to supply its direction and guidance. This is the proper point for the nonintrusive contribution of top management to the early stages of the budgeting process. If well formulated and communicated, the budget will be more responsive, and the reviews more effective and efficient.

Implementing the Strategy/Budget Continuum

The first prerequisite for a strategy/budget continuum is a proper, well-communicated strategy plus plans to carry out that strategy. The budget cannot build on strategy and plans if these are not known clearly by budgeting participants.

A full-blown strategic planning process is not necessary, only desirable. The essential requirements are that (1) the president have a definite strategy, understood and blessed by the board of directors, and (2) the strategy be well communicated to the organization. While participation by others in the organization brings to bear additional and more cogent knowledge, it is possible for the president alone to develop the company's strategy, with only informal inputs from the key people on which he or she depends.

Thus, we must be concerned with the required context for every situation, from a president-generated strategy to the full-blown strategic planning process. For all such situations, there are two key elements in the process design: (1) timing and (2) content.

Timing

Determining the timing for a proper budgeting context in the case of the president-generated strategy is simple: The president must publish and distribute a strategy/plans "white paper" at the beginning of the budgeting process. That is the proper time, certainly no later, and an earlier document allows time for misunderstandings and misinterpretations to arise from particular events.

If the company has a deliberate, participatory strategic planning process, the timing for proper budgeting context is more complicated. Strategic planning generally needs to be divorced from day-to-day problems, or participants will be preoccupied with them. This argues for remoteness in time of strategic planning from budgeting; if done at the same time, all the attention will be on the next year (i.e., the budget) because that involves meaningful measurement. Thus, many companies do their strategic planning during the first and second quarters of the year. The problem with that, however, comes in the associated financial projections: The following year is so far away that optimistic projections will be included in the strategic plan. The participants will be subconsciously confident in their optimism; by budget time, enough outside changes will have occurred that they will be able to get by with budgets that are more pessimistic.

The best solution is to spread the strategic planning over a number of months, planning for the distant future early in the process and only preparing financial projections just before the budgeting process begins. For example, begin the strategic planning in June, finish the qualitative part in August, and then prepare the financial projections so that the entire process is finished by the end of September. This sort of timing, together with the clear communication that the next year's strategic projection is the first cut at next year's budget, will go a long way toward obtaining the desired continuum. Additionally, doing it this way will coincide nicely with a recommendation in Chapter 12: that a preliminary budget be developed early in the budgeting process.

Content

Chapter 8 describes the assumptions process, the first part of which is establishing the pertinent OEFs. These are the factors that significantly influence a company's results and over which it has no control. Since development of the proper OEFs is a major undertaking, and since strategic planning should be outside-in, the ideal time to develop the pertinent OEFs is during the strategic planning process. Carrying these over directly to the budgeting process will ensure the desired strategy/budget continuum for this major dimension. In the case of the president-generated strategy, he or she should still institute a process for developing the pertinent OEFs, because these are needed for budgeting, and this process should be completed before he or she prepares the one-page strategy. Indeed, a participatory process for generating OEFs followed by a one-page strategy prepared by the president would not be a bad strategic planning process by itself.

Gap analysis (see Chapter 11) is a good tool for strategic planning, as it is for budgeting. Gap analysis begins by comparing goals with expectations, which usually defines a "gap." Strategy and plans are then developed for filling this gap. Using gap analysis for both strategic planning and budgeting also helps produce the desired continuum. For the president-generated strategy case, presumably such strategic gap analysis would be done by the president, perhaps with his or her small group of key people.

The gap dimensions—the parameters for which gap analysis will be done—are the company's critical factors for success and improvement, or important problems. The appropriate list of gap dimensions for the budget will be longer than the strategic list. There are always some operationally important issues that should be addressed in the next year that may not be strategically important. Surely, however, all the identified strategically important gap dimensions should also appear in the budgeting process.

Concerning numerical content, the strategic plan should have as few numbers as possible, because it is the thinking about strategy that is important, not the guesses about specific future results. Numerical projections should be in summary form and based on models. Practically, the time period covered by the projections should be the minimum necessary to require thinking beyond current data (again, requiring overcoming preoccupation with day-to-day problems). The maximum period is determined by the time beyond which the OEFs will probably change enough to invalidate any current projections, or the time period in which any endeavors can be influenced by current decisions. It seems that five-year projections are almost standard in American business. But it also seems that three-year projections would be more appropriate for most businesses, particularly since the world seems to change at an ever-faster pace.* Three years is also probably about the minimum to get beyond the preoccupation with day-to-day problems.

This is not meant to imply that there is no place in strategic planning for consideration of the longer-term future. On the contrary, it is useful to attempt to visualize the company far beyond the normal limits of extrapolation and predictability—say, ten or twenty years—as a limiting context for current strategy. However, such long-term analysis should be mainly qualitative, because specific predictions are just guesses. Quantitative long-term analysis should be limited to such statements as, "If we do not believe that we can grow to $x sales in ten years, we should consider selling the company."

In arriving at the numerical content of the strategic plan, most businesses find it useful to base projections on different scenarios. The proper defining basis for the scenarios is largely assumptions regarding the important OEFs. Such a basis is more appropriate than the old "optimistic-realistic-pessimistic" technique because the scenarios are based on the OEFs, which are the real determinants of different scenarios the company may face. The strategy/budget continuum is then automatic: A set of assumptions is chosen for budgeting, and the projection for next year associated with the scenario defined by that particular set of assumptions is then used as the preliminary budget. This also yields an important psychological advantage: Participants are asked to accomplish no more than they already said they could, given those assumptions about the OEFs.

The final item of content that budgeting needs from strategic planning to accomplish the strategy/budget continuum is the one-page strategy statement. Again, this statement summarizes what the company *will* do and what it *will not* do, and it should be mandatory for the budgeting process.

*In some cases, such as telecommunications and forestry companies, current plans are needed to address the far future, decades away. Restriction to three-year projections obviously does not apply to such companies.

Conclusion: The Strategy/Budget Planning Continuum

A strategy/budget continuum must be established to place the budget in its proper strategic context. Similar planning processes, nomenclature, and formats should be used at every step. Activities should be integrated so that there is a logical and natural flow from strategic planning through budgeting. The budget must be consistent with strategy, and budget numbers should be consistent with the numbers in the strategic plan.

If four elements—OEFs, gap dimensions, the one-page strategy statement, and the preliminary numbers—can be established in strategic planning and carried over into the budgeting process, the planning continuum will have been accomplished. That is, the important OEFs, the critical factors for success and the major problems, the strategic "will do's" and "won't do's," and the numbers will be consistent between strategic planning and budgeting.

If formal strategic planning is not done, either at all or in the given year, a "strategy review" must still be done as a prelude to budgeting. In effect, the one-page strategy statement, the OEFs, and the gap dimensions become the first tasks of the budgeting process in this case. They must be done from the company's strategic point of view.

FUNCTIONAL MANAGERS: SURMOUNTING A POOR BUDGETING PROCESS

For a functional manager, the budgeting context is not only the company strategy but also the division strategy and the goals, strategies, and plans of his or her superior and the latter's superiors. We will call this the "strategy/management context."

The relationship of a function's budget to company strategy can range from straightforward to ephemeral, depending on the strategy and the function. A strong new product strategy would directly affect many engineering, manufacturing, and service functions: work content, required skill and knowledge levels, training requirements, processes, and so on. At the other extreme, a strategy to cut back to core businesses would have little or no effect on the manufacturing function of one of the core divisions.

Functional managers are most comfortable if they can relate directly to company strategy, but they must carefully consider the proper context of their planning. They must be most sensitive to their immediate superior and decreasingly sensitive to higher managers, more sensitive to division strategy than to company strategy. A functional manager blunders if he or she budgets large cost increases to handle a stated new product strategy when his or her superior's concentration is actually on improving performance and processes so that more work can be done for the same cost. The superior would not appreciate the justification of a nonresponsive budget by reference to company strategy.

If the strategy/budget continuum does not exist for the company, functional managers need to establish their own. The search for the strategy/ management context should be an inside-out process. It should begin with the function's output dictators and cost drivers, as discussed in Chapter 10 and the Appendix. Functional managers should concentrate on the things that affect their functions; while they should be interested in the rest of the company's strategy, for budgeting they need not worry about elements that do not affect them. If a retail chain suddenly changes strategy from rapidly expanding the number of new stores to promoting growth of existing stores only, the manager charged with obtaining real estate for new stores must reflect this in the budget for it to be meaningful. However, the manager who buys the products to be sold in the stores is not affected much.

Given their output dictators and cost drivers, functional managers should look for strategy/management context items that relate specifically to them. Functional managers should readily be able to learn their immediate superior's goals and plans from direction, discussions, and questions. (They will learn them from the reaction in the first budget review, if not before.) If they have not received guidance on the other elements of context that are important to budgeting, they should estimate them as intelligently as possible. If the manager responsible for real estate in the preceding example cannot learn the company's plans for new stores next year, he or she must estimate the number of new stores. The actual expression of this strategy/ management context in the functional manager's budget should be in terms of assumptions.

In relating their budgets to company or division strategy, there is a trap that functional managers must avoid. Earlier in this chapter, a real example was given of a company president who announced a vigorous growth strategy to his management group, but when budget time came, he cut expenses (particularly marketing expenses) to the bone. It is easy to imagine the trouble functional managers would be in if they budgeted large cost increases to handle the expected growth, while the president was, in fact, looking for sizable expense cuts. Functional managers should not rely on what they hear about strategy; they must see evidence of the strategy being implemented through plans and actions.

If the company's budgeting process does not supply the needed context for functional managers' budgets, they should define it themselves by reasoning from their output dictators and cost drivers to the needs and desires of their superiors to division and company strategies. If something important to an output dictator or cost driver is not known, it should be estimated as intelligently as possible. This strategy/management context is needed for the same reason that the company needs a strategic budgeting context: The functional manager's budget gives meaning to goals, strategies, and plans. Without such a context, the latter have no reality.

8

Dealing With Uncertainty: The Power of Assumptions

A powerful tool in moving the budgeting process toward its objectives and in overcoming the inherent problems is the intelligent use of assumptions. Before preparing the budget, assumptions are made about every important outside environmental factor (OEF). This isolates the uncontrollable aspects of the company's performance, removing them from the iteration and negotiation that accompany all budgeting. In turn, this allows management and the board of directors to focus separately on (1) how the behavior of the outside environment is expected to affect the company over the coming year, and (2) how the company should employ and deploy its resources, resulting in better determination of what management must change and what it must accept. Measurement of management is enhanced by removing uncontrollable items from the measurement criteria, eliminating both windfalls and deficits that result merely from luck.

Briefly, the idea is to (1) identify all the important OEFs that will affect the following year; (2) make the best assumption possible about each of these OEFs; (3) develop the budget numbers based on these assumptions; (4) review these assumptions over the course of the year; and, finally, (5) change the budget and associated measurement if and when it becomes clear that assumptions should be changed.

After the assumptions process is illustrated with a simple example and its benefits explained, the process is discussed step by step.

Assume that a company has a substantial subsidiary in Japan and does a large amount of business there. One of the important OEFs, then, is the yen per dollar relationship. Accounting rules require that the balance sheet be continually revalued in dollars; the value of a balance sheet denominated in yen depends on whether the yen falls or rises against the dollar, generating profits or losses completely outside the control of the company. This currency profit or loss can be significant. Thus, it is appropriate to handle the yen-dollar relationship with a budgetary assumption regarding the average exchange rate for the year in question. The budgeted currency profit or loss is then simply based on this assumption. Any time during the year that there is a large move in the yen versus the dollar, or it is otherwise clear that the assumption will not hold, a new assumption should be made and the budget changed.

How is such an item handled without the assumptions process? To put the predicted profit and balance sheet figures of the Japanese subsidiary in the budget, someone must make an assumption about the yen-dollar rate for the coming year. Typically, however, this assumption is implicit and is not carried with the budget as it progresses to finalization. The Japanese subsidiary profit number is ultimately, then, just part of the budget that management is expected to meet. If during the year the yen-dollar rate is quite different from the assumption (which is probable), management either gets a windfall or has a problem not of its own making. If the latter, there will be pressure to cut some planned, productive activity to get back on budget. In short, the company will be influenced to spend less or more, and management will be rewarded or punished, for an item or event that, in the short term, has no bearing on how well the company is performing. A good strategy may be crippled by cost cuts brought on totally by the outcome of this OEF.

Advantages of the Assumptions Process

The foregoing example is sufficient to illustrate eight important advantages of the assumptions process as a budgeting tool.

1. It makes management and the board of directors focus on the important OEFs that are beyond the company's control. Every company needs to do this, since its destiny is largely controlled by these outside factors, but many find it difficult to do in an organized and effective way.

2. It makes the budget more realistic, the first budgeting objective. Every budgeting participant *must* make assumptions about the OEFs. In the absence of such an assumptions process, they are generally made implicitly, and the assumptions vary from participant to participant. By focusing on them in the beginning and making them uniform and explicit, the company should be able to get both the best possible assumptions and the uniformity needed for realism. Further, hidden pads in budgets are most often motivated by uncertainty about the OEFs; if participants know that these are being treated directly and openly and that the assumptions will change if the OEFs change, there will be much less motivation for hidden pads, one of the main enemies of realism in a budget.

3. It reduces the psychological games of the budgeting process. The playing field is changed, with the superior no longer thinking, "What can I get you to commit?" and the subordinate no longer thinking, "What can I get away with?" (These questions are usually argued on the implicit basis of differing views about OEFs.) The new playing field, for both boss and subordinate, is, "Given the assumed outside conditions, what must *we* do, and what can *we* accomplish?" Laying out relevant assumptions quantitatively and in detail focuses the arguments on concrete reality.

4. It accomplishes the second budgeting objective—a plan for the best results achievable with acceptable risk. By reducing the motivation for hidden pads and reducing the dimensions of the psychological games, the process is more likely to engender submission of an "honest best." Any good manager likes a challenge and will accept one to accomplish more if confident that he or she will not be blindsided by something beyond control.

5. It makes measurement more realistic and fair, both in actuality and perception. By separately focusing on the things that functional managers cannot control, two things are accomplished: They are measured on the things that they can control, but also on their reactions to changes in the outside environment. The latter is so fundamental that it could almost be used as the criterion for good management. With a good assumptions process, management can fairly measure both the case where break-even is good performance in a given year and the case where meeting the budget is really poor performance.

6. It sends an uplifting message to the entire organization that the board of directors and management will focus on, and distinguish between, factors under the organization's control and those not under its control. (The implicit message is that the managers will be measured fairly.) A good manager worries about not being recognized for doing an outstanding job in a year in which the rest of the company does not do well.

7. It provides an excellent role for the board of directors. This is so important that it will be discussed at more length later.

8. It provides an excellent vehicle for understanding, at all levels, the company's critical factors for success. These are the relatively few factors, internal and external, that are the crucial determinants of the company's future. They are something that every company should understand, but they are often difficult to articulate and communicate. The most critical assumptions and OEFs are clearly identified through this process, thus helping the board and management to articulate the internal factors critical for success.

Generating Proper Assumptions

To be useful, the assumptions must be specific enough to show a meaningful cause-and-effect relationship. If a manager is merely asked for budget assumptions with no other preparation, the tendency will be to get assumptions that are either so general as to be useless for the purpose (e.g., "The economy will not go into recession next year") or so specific that they just state what the manager would ordinarily do anyway (e.g, "We will get the budgeted new orders").

The requirements for generating assumptions useful for the budgeting process are that they must relate directly (1) to genuine OEFs and (2) to the business. There will be little value, for example, in an assumption that the gross national product will grow 3 percent next year. GNP growth cannot be related directly to the financial parameters of the business. Imagine the board's reaction if the president were to go to the board in July and propose a reduction in budgeted profit because the GNP is growing at only 1 percent. No one could know whether or not there was a cause-and-effect relationship between the lower GNP growth and the company's lower-than-budget profit. On the other hand, if the company is a manufacturer of major home appliances, the level of housing starts may directly correlate with sales, and it is specific and quantifiable. In that case, the level of housing starts may be the appropriate specific assumption relative to the general economy.

Similarly, inflation is an important economic factor to most businesses, but, again, an assumption about the inflation rate is neither specific nor correlated enough to be useful. The inflation-related assumptions that companies need are about the specific, important elements that affect them, e.g., purchased-material prices, factory entry-wage rate, and fuel costs. (Note that purchased-material prices can be affected by boom or recession, competitive conditions, and so on, as well as inflation, but we do not care. "Purchased material prices" sums up all these OEFs in a specific, measurable factor that directly affects the company's financial parameters.)

An example of an assumption not purely related to OEFs is, "We will keep material costs below 30 percent of sales." This goal is contingent on, among other factors, the type or mix of orders and sales, the price of purchased materials, and factory management factors such as shrinkage and rework. This assumption just baldly states that the submitted budget number will be met.

Because it is difficult to get useful assumptions directly, the proper OEFs should first be determined. With these in hand, the budgeter is focused only on reasonable numbers, rather than on the content itself.

Choosing the Outside Environmental Factors

Development of the pertinent OEFs is a very broad subject. Much market and behavioral research is devoted to it. More than one book could be written on this subject alone. Although direct competitors probably have similar important OEFs, each company will have a somewhat different list. Companies in different industries, geographical locations, or countries will have greatly different lists. Some industries have large bodies of theory, data, and experience on this subject and others have almost none, either because of the inherent nature of the industry, the age of the industry, or just the past attention paid to the subject. If a company or industry has such theory, data, and experience, the budgeter is fortunate and should use it. In many businesses, however, the budgeter will be starting from scratch in determining the OEFs.

The pertinent outside environments were discussed in Chapter 5, and five generalized environments were described: market, industry, economy, government, and financial. To be useful in the budgeting process, the OEFs must be specific and quantifiable, and a direct relationship between them and business results must be demonstrable. While it is appropriate to think about general OEF categories as background, a better approach to developing OEFs is to start with the important financial parameters of the business. This inside-out reasoning is better because it anchors the resulting OEFs to the important numbers of the business. If the assumptions process is started with "inflation," for example, one is forced to think of all the ways inflation may affect the company. Some will probably be overlooked; and anyway, inflation's effect will happen in combination with other things. If, however, the starting point is "expense" or "cash," one is more likely to reason to all the important ways inflation affects the company.

A simplified example will illustrate the inside-out development. Consider a third-party computer maintenance (TPCM) company whose total current-year business consists of ten year-long contracts with industrial customers to manage and maintain all their desktop computing systems. Revenue on each contract increases or decreases as the number of units under management increases or decreases. Assume that one customer accounts for 30 percent of sales, while the others are roughly equal. For most companies, including this one, the fundamental parameters of financial results are (1) sales, (2) expense, and (3) cash.

Next year's sales will be determined by backlog, renewals, and new orders. What OEFs will be important for each of these? Regarding backlog, the company cannot do anything about the number of units under management at a particular customer. This is determined by both the fortunes and the decisions of that customer, which are influenced by the economy, the customer's market and industry, and so on. All those complex and uncertain subjects are not of concern, however; the pertinent factor for the TPCM company relative to backlog is *increase or decrease of customer units under contract*.

For renewals, there are two important factors. The first is the same as for backlog: *increase or decrease of customer units under contract*. More important, however, are whether the customers renew at all, and whether this is beyond the company's control. While management should not be let off the hook if a nonrenewal is the result of poor performance, there are numerous legitimate reasons for nonrenewal that the company cannot influence: a policy decision to minimize outsourcing, a new manager with a favorite vendor, a decision to combine all computer maintenance under one contract with a bigger vendor, and so on. Assume that the only one the board is willing to concede as beyond the company's influence is *customer decisions to combine maintenance contracts under one large vendor*. The OEFs identified must be specific to be useful and to avoid later controversy.

Before considering new orders, one situation in the example TPCM company is noteworthy. (Real, more complex companies will have many special situations.) One customer accounts for 30 percent of sales. Ordinarily, identifying an OEF for single customers leads to hopeless detail, but this one is important enough to justify its own OEF: If something were to happen to this customer, the company could not recover in the short term. The company's concerns relative to the 30 percent customer have many dimensions: the economy, its competition, its financial position, and so on. However, the appropriate OEF sums up all these factors and directly affects the company: *the sales level to the 30 percent customer*. (The associated assumption might later be, if the 30 percent customer is believed to be stable, "Sales to the 30 percent customer will be within plus or minus 10 percent of this year's level.")

As for new orders, this is a business that depends on a small number of (relatively) large orders. Each order is therefore quite important, and the number of prospects is too small for probabilities or statistics to be of much value. What affects new orders that is beyond the company's control? For this example, two factors are considered: *outsourcing decisions by potential customers* and *unusual price cutting by competitors*. (The question of control and influence on orders is controversial and is treated separately in the next section.)

The TPCM company has only two major categories of expense: material and people. Material carries an inherent uncertainty, because it consists of spares and replacement units for equipment that breaks down. This can never be exactly predicted and can result in some big hits to expense, for example, if a large number of units fail in one quarter. Presumably, the TPCM company will be intelligent in using experience and analysis for the related assumption, but this remains a largely uncontrollable expense. Thus, a critical OEF is *customer unit breakdown rate*. There are two more important OEFs related to material, *material price* and *material availability*. The latter refers to an industry-specific factor: Different computer manufacturers have different policies regarding third-party maintainers (whom some manufacturers consider allies, while others consider them competitors), and these policies are sometimes changed and sometimes litigated. A surprise negative policy change could seriously hamper the TPCM company, ranging from increasing its costs by forcing it to secondary sources under unfavorable conditions or by making it impossible to operate for a time.

The company has three important OEFs related to people expense: *ability to hire needed people and associated hiring costs, turnover rate*, and *compensation rate*.

The TPCM company is a low-investment business with good cash flow, so the OEFs here are less critical than for a manufacturer or distributor. The OEFs could be *collection time* and, assuming the company's credit facility expires next year, *bank line renewal* and *associated rates and terms*.

To summarize, thirteen OEFs have been identified, about which assumptions would later be made:

1. Increases or decreases of computer units under contract
2. Customer decisions to combine maintenance contracts under one large vendor
3. The sales level to the 30 percent customer
4. Outsourcing decisions by potential customers
5. Unusual price cutting by competitors
6. Customer unit breakdown rate
7. Material price
8. Material availability
9. Ability to hire needed people, and associated costs
10. Turnover rate
11. Compensation rate
12. Collection time
13. Bank line renewal, and associated rates and terms

In a real case, this list would now probably be revised and pruned. *Material price* is more important to financial results than *collection time*, so the latter might be deleted, for instance.

This simple example is sufficient to illustrate four important points.

1. Useful OEFs are quite company-specific. High-order knowledge, intelligence, and judgment are needed to develop a useful set. No casual outsider can make a list that will fit a particular company.

2. If the budgeting participants are not used to thinking in these terms, choosing the important OEFs will not be easy. Any real company is more complex than the simplified TPCM example. However, very little in management is ever easy; the right question is whether it is worthwhile.

3. There is clear value in merely developing this list, even if nothing else is done, particularly if it is thoroughly communicated up and down the management hierarchy and to the board of directors. The benefits are a better understanding of the company's critical factors for success and of the things that can be changed and those that must be accepted.

4. A better budget for the TPCM company would result if the above OEFs were refined with assumptions. In the absence of this, how would management handle the inherent uncertainty of material expense? Most managers would understand that they would be measured on *all* expense, would use analysis and experience to estimate material expense in a normal year, and then would add a large pad to this item in case of a possible atypical year of excessive equipment failures. The result of this padded material expense? The budget will not show the best results achievable, and there will be a possible windfall of above-budget performance if there is not excessive equipment failure. Thus, managers will either be rewarded or punished merely for luck plus the degree of conservatism they were allowed in the review process.

The Controversial OEFs for New Orders

The TPCM company example is sufficiently realistic to illustrate that OEFs for any company can be controversial. It is easy to see that the yen versus dollar rate, or interest rates, or a new government regulation, is beyond the control of the company. For the categories of cash, expense, and sales, however, the OEFs are often not so obvious. It takes effort, understanding, and negotiation to agree on proper factors that are really outside management's control and influence.

The biggest problem in defining and using OEFs is generally for new orders. Some argue that the problems associated with new orders are the reason large sales commissions are paid. In other words, salespersons are paid to fight through and influence things not under their control. Others argue that new orders are mostly luck and are uncontrollable. Both are right in different circumstances. (Orders have little or no meaning in any cash business, including almost all retail businesses. The customer comes in and either buys or does not buy. There is no contract to have something made or built or done in the future. However, as generally the most complex OEF subject, orders are a good vehicle for illustrating the problem of OEF complexity and its treatment.)

Some businesses really cannot influence orders very much.

That may sound heretical; businesses exist to identify and serve customers, and a large consulting industry is based on convincing customers to order particular products or services. Still, there are businesses and industries in which a product *cannot* be sold; it must be bought.

Contrast a business that sells computers to military buyers with a new car dealership. In the latter, good marketing may entice customers into the showroom, and then good salesmanship may convince them to buy a car a year earlier than they had planned. The computer company, on the other hand, may market and sell to the point that the potential customers are convinced that Western civilization might fall unless they get their hands on the computer. However, the company will not get one order from those prospects unless a particular government program is approved for which the computer could be used and the cost justified. And the decision to approve a particular military program is totally independent of anything that the computer company could do.

This particular example has recently become reality. When the cold war suddenly ended in late 1989, the U.S. military research and development budget was thrown into disarray. It was not that programs were immediately canceled but that so much uncertainty surrounded so many of them that program plans and capital purchases were put on hold. Anyone selling computers to the military R&D establishments and their contractors suddenly was getting no orders. Because this happened quickly and was not predicted, it would be improper to blame the general manager of a military computer division for missing the orders budget during that period: The pertinent outside environment had changed, surprising everyone. (That general manager should be blamed if he or she did not quickly react to curtail expenses and capital expenditures, but that is another story.) Thus, there are genuine cases in which orders cannot be obtained because of OEFs.

Another dimension of identifying OEFs for new orders arises because the budgeting problems of businesses with few big orders are quite different from those with many small orders. I call these "hockey and basketball" businesses. In hockey games (businesses), sometimes the team does everything right, but the goalie knocks the puck aside and no goal (order) is scored. However, one needs very few goals to win the game (achieve good sales). Conversely, in basketball games (businesses), no single basket (order) is very important, but one has to get a large number of them to win.

The budgeting problem is clearly different for the two types. In a "basketball" business, one can use probabilities, statistics, trends, and experience to relate orders to marketing and sales effort. In a "hockey"-type business, a few orders can make or break the year and cause wide variations in needed expense and cash.

Thus, not surprisingly, there are great variations among different types of businesses relative to the controllability and importance of particular orders. Clearly, though, most businesses have some definable cases in which the level of new orders is properly an OEF, something management cannot do much about. The trick is for top management and the board of directors to correctly define these.

The TPCM company example developed two OEFs for new orders: *outsourcing decisions by potential customers* and *unusual price cutting by competitors.* Both illustrate potential controversy. The board of directors may say that management is paid to sell the concept of outsourcing. On the other hand, if a potential customer's management suddenly decides at a policy level to eliminate outsourcing, there may be nothing that the TPCM company can do to change that decision. Similarly, "unusual price cutting" is the extreme type of price cutting involved in "buying in" to an industry. Whether or not this is an OEF is arguable almost every time it happens, and some directors will suspect that the problem is just that the company's costs are too high. There is always discomfort in hearing someone wail that the competition is unfair, but there are also times when the board should not want the company to meet a competitor's price.

The solution to this complexity of OEFs for new orders must come from the specific business situation and the knowledge of it held by top management and the board. Some companies undoubtedly should have no budget-changing OEFs related to orders. This is, in fact, a chief area in which management sometimes tries to wriggle off the hook of commitment, and salespersons are good advocates for a decision favorable to them (or else they would not be good salespersons). However, many types of companies deal with uncontrollable environments concerning orders, and it is unrealistic to pretend otherwise. One is tempted to generalize that the more the company is a "hockey" business and the more it cannot influence at least the timing of an order, the more valid OEFs for orders there will be. But, again, all OEFs depend on the specific business situation, and effort, intelligence, and understanding are required to properly identify them.

Even if difficult, budgeting will be improved if intelligent efforts are made to identify factors on which management should be measured and important OEFs that it cannot control or influence. There is value in going through the process, even if no one is fully satisfied with the results. Results will improve as the process is continued year to year. Determining OEFs for orders and for other controversial areas, and doing it rigorously so life is not made too easy for management, will add value to the budgeting process.

From Assumptions to Budget to Review

With the important OEFs determined, the statement of assumptions is the straightforward, intelligent choice of words and numbers to describe how each OEF is expected to behave in the following year.

Some assumptions should be given considerable time and effort, while others deserve very little. While the OEFs selected and their related assumptions should all be important for *financial results* by definition, assumptions differ greatly in importance from the point of view of *management action*. The yen versus dollar rate discussed in an earlier example was important financially but surely would result in no short-term action. Therefore, the magnitude of any related assumption is not very important, and little time and effort should be spent on it.

Assumptions regarding markets, competition, particular important customers, particular costs, and the like are essential elements of management's plans. Unlike the yen versus dollar rate assumption, these should be the result of extensive thought and work. The necessary context for the budget is discussed in Chapter 7. The assumptions should be consistent with, and based on, the judgments used in formulating strategy and plans. If strategy and plans have been formulated well and expressed explicitly, the words and numbers for the budgeting assumptions should be fairly obvious. If they are implicit, the assumptions process gives another benefit: It will help make the strategy judgments explicit. Conversely, reexamining the strategic planning process vis-à-vis the budgeting assumptions will provide good feedback as to the logic and consistency of the strategy and action plans.

There is again no cookbook approach to articulating budgeting assumptions. As in most management activities, one must apply the best intelligence, knowledge, experience, data, and intuition available.

How important is it that the budgeting assumptions turn out to be correct? The answer varies from assumption to assumption. It is important that the assumptions that influence management action be reasonable, because the company is probably staking its future on the judgments that led to these assumptions. It is not important whether such assumptions as the yen-dollar rate are correct; the experts who forecast this relationship as part of their profession are often wrong, so why should we expect to be right?

But the initial question, "How important is it that the budgeting assumptions turn out to be correct?" misses the point. The reason assumptions are used is that the budget must deal with future uncertainty about uncontrollable factors. In the narrow sense of the budget for the next year (as opposed to the broad sense of company direction and strategy for the long term), it is not important whether the assumptions are correct. The important things are the thought that goes into making the assumptions and articulating them and the value of the continual review process in both directing the company and measuring management.

Bank interest rates illustrate these points about the correctness of assumptions. The available interest rate spread between borrowing and lending can be crucial for a bank and is fundamental to lending strategy. However, the underlying rates themselves—the prime rate, Federal Reserve rates, and so on—are beyond the bank's control and should be the subject of assumptions. It would seem important for the bank to make the correct assumption for next year on something so important.

However, because interest rates are so inherently unpredictable, it would clearly be imprudent to adopt a strategy that "bets the bank" on a given interest-rate prediction. The most important thing, then, is for the bank to react quickly to changes in interest rates, not to be right initially, which would be largely lucky. Explicit assumptions allow a business to continuously monitor the important OEFs and trace the effects of OEF changes through the budget and the business. Thus, the value is not in the correctness of the initial assumption, but in the way the assumptions facilitate management in the face of surprises.

The assumptions also facilitate preparation of the budget, which should flow straightforwardly and consistently from them. Then, the budgets pass through their multiple levels of review, culminating with review of the overall company budget by the board of directors. The assumptions should occupy a good portion of the review at every level. Once these are agreed on (and known to be assumptions subject to change), the review can unambiguously and directly focus on the things under management's control: work content, resources required, time required, capital expenditures needed, new procedures required, and so on. Clearly, this will be a more fruitful review than the "can so, can not" arguments that flow from statements such as, "I do not think you will need twenty more people, because the economy is going to be poor next year."

A good starting point for developing assumptions is at the division level. These assumptions should be reconciled with companywide assumptions first developed by the chief financial officer (or with groupwide assumptions for very large companies). These should then be reviewed and compared by the president and all the division general managers and corporate staff vice-presidents. When an agreed-on set of assumptions is obtained at the top level, the assumptions should be promulgated downward. Questions and alternative suggestions should be solicited from functional managers. After any budget iteration that results, the assumptions should be finalized and the budgeting should proceed.

What? Change the Budget?

The company may well not meet its original budget using this process. In fact, the original budget might be changed a number of times throughout the year. Again, the point is to continually and realistically keep track of, and react to, the OEFs, *not* to assume that the company will be accurate about the OEFs at least one year in advance.

How about the opposite problem: If the company keeps changing the budget, will it not clearly meet the budget every year, making measurement meaningless? The answer is no, and this is why the review process and the role of the disinterested board of directors (discussed in the section following the next section) is so important. The process must operate so that only appropriate assumption modifications are allowed to change the budget; it cannot let assumptions be changed to hide poor performance. Consider an example in which, during the year in question, the design of a product must be changed, making it more expensive to build. The assumptions process requires that the reason for the change be reviewed. If the change is the result of poor performance because of the original design, no change in assumptions and budget should be made. On the other hand, if the change must be made because of a new and unanticipated government safety regulation, an assumption and budget change is probably appropriate. People should not be punished for the whims of the government, and they will appreciate the fact that they are not.

This appears to violate a sacred cow of business: that the budget should never be changed. Guilty as charged. The point is that this particular sacred cow is counterproductive, because it does not recognize the unpredictability of the outside environment. It assumes that management has everything under its control and can do anything it wants, if it is just smart enough. This is just not true, and many bad decisions are made in many companies every year—most often by doing something bad for the long term in the hopes of fixing a short-term budget deficit—because of this dictum that budgets should be inviolate. Further, in the computer age, it is simple to keep the original budget available as a "stake in the ground." This revision trail will give the added benefit of supplying a quantitative history of the specific events that have affected the company.

Everyone agrees that businesses must operate in an environment of ever-accelerating change. It is time to use the available information technology to track that change, rather than expecting budgets to be cast in concrete.

Another Benefit: Assimilation of an Acquired Business

The New division of the fictitious QRS Company (Chapters 2 and 3) offers an illustration of another benefit that can be obtained from the assumptions process: aid in assimilation of an acquired business.

New had been acquired by QRS during the current year, and its division general manager (DGM) had three main budgeting problems. First, he had no confidence that New could achieve the projections for next year, which he had made to support the acquisition. Second, he knew the president of QRS did not understand New's business in detail. Third, he and his staff were overwhelmed by the large demands of the QRS financial people for unfamiliar supporting data to accompany the budget.

The way the assumptions process can work to overcome such problems is as follows. The president of QRS sets up a two- or three-day meeting off-site whose purpose is to define important OEFs for New. Attendees are the QRS president, the QRS chief financial officer, the New DGM, and his key management team. The president can lead the meeting himself or bring in a facilitator to do so. The first half day, roughly, is spent getting the New management team familiar with the OEFs/assumptions concept and with thinking about the outside world in the needed fashion. (A good way to do this is to have a free-flowing, noncritical discussion of the five basic OEF categories noted in Chapter 5: market, industry, economy, government, and financial.) The rest of the meeting is focused upon defining the specific uncontrollable OEFs that affect New's performance in important ways. The last step in the meeting should be a first cut at budgeting assumptions, again to get everyone familiar with the concept. However, the finalizing of assumptions should await considerable investigative work by New people after the meeting.

The benefits that could be obtained from such a meeting are:

- The important OEFs for New are defined.

• The QRS president and chief financial officer understand New's business much better, from the concentrated discussion of the important factors affecting New.

• QRS and New key people know and understand each other better, both from the meeting and from socializing in the evening (the latter is the reason for having the meeting off-site). After such a meeting, the communication in both directions should improve.

• The New DGM can take the opportunity outside the meeting to discuss the "unreasonable" supporting data requirements with the QRS chief financial officer. The DGM will either understand those requirements better or get them reduced. The QRS chief financial officer will understand that some of the data do not apply to New's business and start to define different data that company management needs from New.

• The meeting provides a good setting for the New DGM to "take his medicine" and admit that his preacquisition projections were too optimistic. This fact will be confirmed by future events in any case. By facing the issue at such a meeting, he clears the air and brings himself and the QRS president together as two people who need to work the same problem. They can both then address the best course of action for increasing New's value (helped by focusing on the OEFs, the best parameters, and problems and goals through gap analysis).

There are potential traps in this approach, which lie in the possible insecurity and resulting game-playing of the participants in this relationship. Both the QRS president and the New DGM must recognize this and behave accordingly. The New people will probably have to be coaxed to open up in the meeting. The QRS president must check his power position at the door, encourage free discussion, and not dominate the meeting. He must remember that he is probably an awesome figure to the New people, particularly to those who have never before dealt with the president of a company as large as QRS.

The New DGM must also recognize his role as a participant and not dominate his people. He must get into the spirit of free-flowing discussion. He must not be afraid of looking stupid, or having his people look stupid, in front of the QRS president. His purpose cannot be to have his people look good or say what the president wants to hear. He and his people must not play games; their purposes for the meeting must be the straightforward ones of learning a useful tool, helping New's management process, and improving communications.

As president of two different multidivision organizations, I used such meetings with great benefit, particularly with new acquisitions and new vice-presidents. However, I did fall into a trap on one occasion. At a meeting, I could never draw out the division people to generate a heated discussion. After the meeting I learned that the DGM had brought his people together before the meeting to develop a consensus and to coach them on what and what not to say in my presence. However, even if the group falls into a trap, nothing will be lost except time. (Even in this personal trap, I learned something useful about that DGM, although he probably did not learn much about me.) If the meeting goes well, the benefits can be considerable.

The assumptions process—and particularly the development of the OEFs—is an ideal vehicle for such a meeting.

A Powerful Role for the Board of Directors

Another benefit of the assumptions process is that it provides an excellent role for the board of directors. That boards of directors are not as effective as they should be is considered a problem in corporate America these days. Much has been written on the subject, and, unfortunately, alleged deficiencies of boards of directors find their way into more and more lawsuits.

The cures are worse than the disease if they focus on involving the board more in the company's day-to-day affairs, as they often do. Typical directors spend a day or two per month on company business—not nearly enough to manage the company. Yet, having directors spend enough time to be effective as managers would be either prohibitively expensive to the company or impossible for busy directors. It would require that only retired people be made directors; even then, there would be the problem of multiple people conning the ship, which confuses people and invites disaster.

The assumptions process, however, involves the board of directors in a way ideally suited to the contribution that it can make. Outside directors are substantial people, chosen for their intelligence, accomplishments, and extensive knowledge of business, government, technology, and the like. Collectively, they should possess the broad perspective that the nose-to-the-grindstone management often lacks. Thus, the board of directors is the ideal review body for the assumptions when they are first made. Further, the budget assumptions are an excellent vehicle for a strategic discussion of the business between the board and management.

The budgeting assumptions are also an excellent vehicle to assist the board of directors in discharging its responsibilities of corporate governance without engaging in micromanagement. Directors are not the people to overhaul a problem purchasing function, for example; if outside help is needed, the company should hire a consultant, who probably will have to work full-time for months on the assignment. If presented with assumptions and budget numbers representing work, costs, and resources, however, directors should be able to observe that, for example, (1) material costs seem high, given the purchased material price assumption that has been made, or (2) more action needs to be taken relative to an anticipated shortage of an important purchased part. Thus, the directors are made aware of a problem without micromanaging and then are alert to monitor that problem and management's reaction to it.

Directors are also in the best position to question whether the OEFs are legitimate. For example, either from experience or from general knowledge and intelligence, a director may validly question, at a particular time for a particular company, whether purchased material prices are really beyond management's control. He or she may feel strongly that the purchasing people should be able to keep total material costs down. The burden of proof is on management to justify that its selected OEFs are truly beyond its control, or to modify the wording to capture the aspect that is truly an OEF.

The board has another major contribution to make. It is an essential part of the assumptions process to review the assumptions throughout the year. It will be tempting for some managements at times to change assumptions to cover poor performance. A disinterested review body, outside of management, is the final control essential to the success of the process. Clearly, the board should have the final decision concerning whether assumptions, and therefore the budget, should be changed.

The assumptions process also aids the board in discharging what is arguably its greatest responsibility: measuring management. Since the assumptions are a deliberate attempt to distinguish between controllable and uncontrollable factors, they clarify management's performance in both managing controllable factors and reacting to surprises in uncontrollable factors. Management performance can thus be more confidently and objectively measured and judged.

It should be clear that the board of directors must be a party to the budgeting process from the very beginning. The board must agree to exercise this review role, which may require it to eschew other roles and pursue a new mode of operation. This will generally require some persuasion by the president, but it is worth the effort.

Conclusion

When a budget is indiscriminately made up of items that management can control and items it cannot, and then cast in concrete, the budget is considerably less valuable than it could be. The budgeting objectives of all participants are more closely approached, and budgeting problems reduced, if budgeting is begun with the assumptions process. In this process, assumptions identify and describe important factors over which the company has no control or influence, allowing top management and the board of directors to focus separately on the pertinent outside factors and management performance.

Useful assumptions are company-specific and take effort, intelligence, knowledge, and understanding. A good starting point is the identification of important OEFs. The appropriate place to begin is generally the division level, iterating upward, then downward, and again upward in the management chain, until finalized. The assumptions are then the best available for each OEF, and they are directly inserted into the budget. Budget reviews at all levels then focus separately on the assumptions—the outside environment—and on how the company should employ and deploy its resources.

As the budget year progresses, assumptions are reviewed and changed when a significant change in an OEF occurs that invalidates an assumption. A key part of the process is that the budget is then changed as well. The point is to continually and realistically keep track of, and react to, the OEFs, *not* to expect that the company will be accurate about the OEFs at least one year in advance. While some may object to changing the budget, everyone agrees that businesses must operate in an environment of ever-accelerating change. Companies should use the available information technology to let the budget track that change, rather than adhere to a budget that is unrealistic yet inflexible.

In the process, the key role of final arbiter on when it is appropriate to change assumptions is held by the board of directors. The board, with its general experience and broad perspective, should be ideally suited to this role, and it is necessary for the integrity of the process to have a disinterested body make these decisions. An important side benefit is that this deepens the involvement of the board of directors in the company's affairs in a particularly appropriate way, increasing the value of the board's contribution to the health of the company.

FUNCTIONAL MANAGERS: SURMOUNTING A POOR BUDGETING PROCESS

Use of the assumptions process by a functional manager on his or her own, when the company or division does not use it, can confer both major benefits and major difficulties. The benefits are the same as for a company using it: understanding and rational treatment (in the budget and in management) of the organization's important uncontrollable factors, plus limitation of the scope of the psychological games inherent in budgeting.

The primary difficulty is that, in a poor process, a changed assumption by the functional manager will not be accepted as a reason to change the budget. A second difficulty is that the assumptions process for a function has more dimensions than that for a company, and the dimensions must be carefully differentiated. The company process is concerned only with OEFs, since the company controls its strategy and decisions about employment and deployment of its resources. A function, on the other hand, controls few of the things that determine its outputs and costs. The entire strategy/management context is beyond the functional manager's control.

Additionally, some important elements of the way the company does business are beyond the functional manager's influence or control, but careful distinctions must be made here. Things dictated in other parts of the company are appropriate material for assumptions. However, plans and actions for the department or division in which the function resides require input from the functional manager. Therefore, assumptions are not appropriate for schedules, processes, procedures, and so forth, by which the department or division gets its work done. Consider a purchasing manager in a manufacturing department. The number of new products for next year is a part of the strategy/management context and appropriate for an assumption. The purchasing manager has no control and little influence over benefits costs (partly an OEF and partly a top-management decision, recommended by human resources), so an assumption would also be appropriate here. However, an assumption regarding required inventory levels would be inappropriate; part of the purchasing manager's job is to work with other manufacturing functions and with suppliers to find ways to minimize inventory.

For the assumptions process, the uncontrollable factors for the functional manager arising from the strategy/management context plus company decisions made remotely from him or her are referred to as internal uncontrollable factors (IUFs). Functional manager assumptions are appropriate for IUFs as well as OEFs. In identifying IUFs, the functional manager should be particularly careful not to include assumptions about things that can be construed to be controllable in his or her job; if the concept of such assumptions in budgeting is unfamiliar to his or her superiors, the functional manager could be accused of game playing. The intent should be to get the concept accepted, leading to wider use; the functional manager should not attempt anything marginal that could invite negative reactions.

In the absence of a company or division assumptions process, functional managers should conduct their own. They can do it alone but, if their style and conditions permit, will get more benefit from involving their key people and superiors, if possible. The process should be inside-out. First, the output dictators and cost drivers important for the function are determined. Then, which of these are important OEFs and IUFs is decided and assumptions are made for them. These assumptions are then stated prominently as part of the budget, and related budget numbers come directly from them.

The purchasing manager in a manufacturing department can again be used to illustrate the process. In considering the output dictators and cost drivers, the purchasing manager divides his responsibility into two parts: procurement of direct material for the factory, and "all other" procurement as a service to the entire division. Working with his key buyers and with input from his superior, the purchasing manager develops the following list of the main determinants of outputs and costs for the factory procurement portion of his responsibility:

- Type, amount, and schedule of products to be produced (from the sales budget and planning's schedule)
- Supplier prices (the cost of direct material is part of the purchasing manager's budget)
- The required level of inventory relative to production, determined by manufacturing policies and processes
- The amount of expediting that must be done (determined by supplier performance; changes in product type, amount, or schedule; and timely and correct purchase orders)
- The amount of reordering that must be done, resulting from bill-of-material changes, which in turn results from engineering change notices (ECNs)
- The degree of automation of purchasing's work and information system (assume that changes must be done by management information systems (MIS), which reports to finance)
- Personnel costs factors: average salary increase, benefits costs, hiring costs and salaries

The purchasing manager concludes that his responsibility for procurement service to the rest of the company is mainly driven simply by the number of purchase orders. (The cost of the material purchased goes against the budgets of the purchasing manager's "customers" and so is not relevant to the purchasing budget.) From experience, the purchasing manager knows that these service requirements are small, handled by his people essentially in slack time. Although the "all other" procurement requirements are an appropriate subject for an assumption, the purchasing manager decides they are not important enough to mention.

In the foregoing list of output and cost determinants, the OEFs are supplier prices, supplier performance, output and schedule changes resulting from customer actions that the company is unable to influence, part of benefits costs, and labor market conditions affecting hiring costs and salaries. Appropriate IUFs are the sales budget, output and schedule changes decided outside manufacturing (i.e., by top management, marketing, or engineering), the number of ECNs, the agreement and performance of MIS in making changes in the level of automation, and part of benefits costs. The purchasing manager is expected to influence and contribute to the other things on the list.

The first information the purchasing manager wants from the list is the inputs that he needs from others to prepare his budget: factory production plan, an MIS automation commitment if significant changes are planned, the average salary increase, and expected benefits costs. He would also like to know how many ECNs and output/schedule changes to expect, but probably cannot get a definitive answer to these questions. The purchasing manager must develop the rest of the information in conjunction with colleagues in manufacturing.

In deciding which items to treat with assumptions, the purchasing manager needs to use knowledge of his job and of his superior and the company. If the purchasing manager is introducing the assumptions process for the first time, he probably wants to keep the assumptions to a minimum. There is no need to state assumptions for things everybody knows are necessary inputs to purchasing, e.g., production schedule, average salary increase, and benefits costs.

The first three items in the list are the major determinants of purchasing's costs. Within these items, supplier prices are the only element both obviously uncontrollable and important, and so appropriate for an assumption. If unexpected schedule changes, from either the customer or from marketing, have been important in the past, an assumption about them is also appropriate. Similarly, if frequent ECNs have resulted in considerable purchasing costs to change purchase orders and expedite material, that should also have an assumption. If a major change in automation of purchasing's work or information system is planned, an assumption should be presented regarding the schedule and quality of the automation. Thus, in this example, the purchasing manager could end up with four assumptions, the subjects being supplier prices, number of output and schedule changes, number of ECNs, and the scheduled availability and quality of a planned automation change.

This example illustrates the extensive benefits of the assumptions process, together with its proper context, for the purchasing manager. Functional managers control so little of their job that they often feel they are just reacting to events designed to complicate their lives. Some of that is unavoidable, but look how the purchasing manager benefits by going through the assumptions process:

- The purchasing manager, key people in the department, and presumably the purchasing manager's superior understand their jobs better because of concentrated attention to their output dictators and cost drivers.

- By understanding what is controllable and uncontrollable about their jobs, they are able to focus their talents on things they can change.
- By thinking things through in this fashion, they can have the best budget possible under the circumstances.
- Knowing that their work will be subject to many changes throughout the year, the purchasing manager now knows what changes will have important effects and to what factors he must react. He can stay alert for the important changes and not get excited about changes that will not affect the organization.

The primary difficulty remains, however. In a poor budgeting process, the functional manager can expect no budget relief from a changed assumption. In other words, while the manager recognizes the subject of the assumption as an uncontrollable factor, the company's budgeting process does not so recognize it. This difficulty cannot be removed, but it can be reduced. First, the functional manager should communicate fully and carefully with his or her superior, with the latter's superior, and with accounting. The manager should get these people to understand what is uncontrollable about the job, even if the budgeting process does not recognize it. Second, the manager should pad the budget to allow for more negative manifestations of the OEFs and IUFs than has been assumed. Such a practice was decried earlier, but the company's poor budgeting process leaves no choice here. Assumptions, after all, are about uncontrollable things, and the manager must protect himself or herself and the function's budget. Third, if the superior's style and personality allow it, the functional manager should present everything that has been done factually and objectively, including the pads and their reasons. The manager wants to influence the superior and colleagues to move toward better budgeting and better management; he or she needs a reputation for objectivity and honesty to do this. (Devious people do not often get management processes changed to their benefit, unless they are very good at being devious.)

9

Selecting the Format:
The Best Parameters

For good management, the company must focus on its most important financial parameters. The budget format can be either the cause or the effect of the process that identifies and develops the most useful information, but the result is the same: The way the budget presents information is the way information will be addressed throughout the year. Thus, the proper information format is a major requirement of the budgeting process.

What is the "most useful information for management," the third composite budgeting objective identified in Chapter 4? It is the information that allows all levels of management to determine the profitability, benefits, and consequences of their various activities. This in turn provides a proper basis for analysis of the benefits and consequences of proposed actions, or lack of action. That is, the most useful information is that which best allows management to understand the company's financial driving forces and critical success factors. The proper vehicle for illuminating these forces and factors is the budget format: the most important parameters must be selected for focus and emphasis.

A Focus on Profit, Cash, and Activities

If a woman starts a candy and ice cream store, on what should she focus? She will surely be most interested in cash flow, the first-order survival parameter of any business, large or small.

If she is energetic and deliberate about maximizing that cash flow, she will want to know how much it costs her to sell candy and to sell ice cream, both to find ways to reduce costs and to decide possibly to emphasize one more than the other. The most natural way to do this is to identify the *activities* involved in each—the particular things that must be *done* to sell candy and to sell ice cream. Aggregating costs into functions like purchasing and sales will not indicate the cash obtained from candy versus that obtained from ice cream. Grouping rent, utilities, advertising, and taxes into one cost number and then allocating it to candy and ice cream in proportion to their sales will not help either; storage and electricity costs for ice cream will be high relative to candy. The way to get visibility into cash flow from candy versus ice cream is to understand what it costs to buy, store, display, and sell each—the *activities* involved.

Ten years later, when the candy and ice cream store has become the hugely successful public Goodies, Inc., with $500 million in annual sales, two things will have happened. The first is that the company will now focus on profit more than cash flow. Public companies (and private companies that need to borrow money or want to compare themselves to competitors) are mostly measured on profit. There is a long history of accounting theory and practice, expressed as generally accepted accounting principles (GAAP), that prescribes profit as a better measure of a company's health than cash flow. (GAAP are sometimes controversial, and profit can be managed in the short term, but that is another story.) Knowing that cash is still the first-order parameter, the former owner, now president and largest stockholder, will work to focus the company on both profit and cash flow.

The second thing that will have happened is that the business is now organized by function (e.g., purchasing, marketing, operations, real estate); naturally, considerable organization is needed to manage the many employees and product lines of a company of this size. Unfortunately, costs are now aggregated by function, and various ratios are used to allocate costs and measure the results of the different product lines. Instead of directly knowing the activities that determine profit and cash flow, the president now employs a staff to analyze these aggregate costs and ratios. It is now difficult to determine the profitability of different product lines and to identify the important costs that can and should be reduced. Also, her managers are measured on functional costs and on the various ratios used to measure results, so they naturally focus on these "third order" parameters rather than on profit and cash. She wonders why her job is not as much fun anymore.

This little fable illustrates what is needed from the budget format to provide the most useful information for management. First, the format must emphasize profit and cash flow directly and focus management's attention on total cost rather than burden rates and ratios. Second, the format must relate business outputs—products delivered and services rendered, expressed as sales—to the *activities* that contribute to, and are required by, those outputs. Activities are what an organization *does*; they drive costs, and knowing the activities involved in a given business output is the only way to fully know the profitability of that output.

Activities are also a principal basis developed by Harvard Business School Professor and Management Consultant Michael Porter to determine competitive advantage:

> Competitive advantage cannot be understood by looking at a firm as a whole. It stems from the many discrete activities a firm performs in designing, producing, marketing, delivering, and supporting its product. . . . A systematic way of examining all the activities a firm performs and how they interact is necessary for analyzing the sources of competitive advantage.[1]

Porter calls the tool for doing such analysis the *value chain*. Clearly, focusing on activities for making the budget a better planning and management tool is closely related and can facilitate Porter's strategic analysis.

In a business of any size, it is almost impossible to relate every activity rigorously to an output; there are too many general support activities and too many things that do not vary linearly with output. However, the principle of diminishing returns operates: It is ordinarily sufficient to relate only the high-cost and highly variable activities to outputs. Complete management infor-

---

1. Michael E. Porter, *Competitive Advantage* (New York: The Free Press, 1985).

mation is an impossible goal in any case. More good information is always better than less, and the most and best data available should be used for any important decision. Perfection is not required for improvement over current practices. As said a number of times in this book, in budgeting incremental gain can always be obtained from incremental effort.

To address proper budget format, then, this chapter presents techniques that can increase management's knowledge of and emphasis on the parameters of activities and outputs and their relationships, which determine profit and cash flow. But first, the main sources of budget format problems are further discussed.

Sources of Format Problems

There are two principal sources of budget format problems, and they are closely related. The first is tradition.

Traditional Methods

Traditional accounting and budgeting methods were designed for a precomputer world in which information was difficult to acquire. These methods often obscure rather than clarify the financial driving forces and critical success factors. A large segment of the business world budgets and manages in terms of direct and indirect costs and various burden rates—overhead rates, general and administrative (G&A) expense rates, and so on. In manufacturing, a force behind this is the accounting requirement to value work-in-progress inventory. Most businesses that do work for the federal government are forced by procurement practices to bill in terms of similar direct and indirect costs and burden rates. Public utility accounting drives utilities in the same direction.*

*Businesses that do not have these accounting, billing, or rate-making characteristics—retail, financial services, distribution, for instance—are fortunate to be free of these obscuring factors. However, tradition still operates to make such businesses accumulate a variety of expenses in a few large categories, without an attempt to relate them to business outputs and activities. Without useful information on financial drivers from their company's "system," managers tend to manage on artificial, partial proxies for cost drivers, such as controlling head count. If a bank, for example, controls the number of employees to contain costs, managers who need more work done will use consultants or subcontractors instead of hiring people. The frequent result is higher total cost.

The traditional methods would be all right if, for example, all indirect labor were really incurred in proportion to direct labor on different projects, which typical manufacturing and engineering overhead rates imply; or if G&A expense were really incurred in proportion to overall sales or cost of sales. However, this is hardly ever the case. The result is a blunt tool of little use in relating business outputs to their critical driving forces.

The use of burden rates can focus management attention on the wrong financial parameters. Consider a factory deciding whether to outsource one of the functions it currently performs. The right financial question is, "Will total cost for a given output be reduced?" Now, outsourcing work always reduces direct labor, and so always increases the manufacturing overhead rate. If manufacturing overhead rate is a prominent budget and measurement parameter, manufacturing and accounting people focus on it, rather than total cost. That right question might never be asked, and a good and proper outsourcing decision might never be made.

Similarly, if budgeting and measurement focus on overhead rates and other such ratios, employees may develop the unhealthy attitude that "direct cost is good, indirect cost is bad," when the organization should be working to minimize all costs. (This kind of thinking can even affect the accountants, who should know better. For example, when I joined one company, the customer service manager was doing a great job and was well below budget in both direct and indirect labor on fixed-price contracts. Because he was further below budget in direct labor, however, his overhead rate was above budget. Accounting—and I am not making this up—was telling him to increase his direct labor so that his overhead rate would go down.)

There is nothing fundamental in the distinction between direct and indirect expense, although this is deeply ingrained in business practice. Indeed, such terminology for labor carries with it the implication that direct people are the important "paddlers," while indirect people are "passengers." The business world continuously moves toward a higher proportion of indirect labor. As a factory automates, assembly workers (direct) are replaced by engineers and technicians (indirect). As equipment evolves, maintenance service businesses reduce repair technicians (direct) and add material management people (indirect). The distinction between direct and indirect labor is not only becoming less meaningful, it is becoming a hindrance in ascertaining total costs of a product or service.

Default

Surprising as it may seem, many companies' budgeting processes do not even appear to address the issue of usefulness of information in managing the business. I have seen a number of budgets and corresponding monthly financial reports expressed in the same terms as the annual report—the line items are "sales," "cost of sales," "gross profit," "selling, general and administrative expense," and so on. I have seen others in which there is only a first-level breakdown of sales and cost of sales, but, under expense, there are separate line items for minor things like office supplies and postage. Still others include pages and pages of numbers, but most functional managers need to get out pencil and paper to derive the numbers they need.

The source of the problem is that the format of the budget is often designed to be consistent with the way the books are kept and the financial statements are prepared. This is the wrong way. The budget, and all the control and management reviews and techniques that proceed from the budget, are tools of management, not of accounting or financial reporting.

In many companies, the accountant's information system is the only one that exists. The accountants recognized the need for automated information long ago, while some managers are just now getting to the subject of management information systems. For the budget to fulfill its potential as a planning and management tool, a true management information system must be addressed. This can be an overwhelming major task, or it can be a step-by-step process of experimentation and incremental improvement. The latter is generally recommended, since *knowledge* of the best information seems to grow with *use* of better information.

There should be no concerns about budget data being in different terms from financial reporting data. With information technology what it is today, it is easy to convert management information to accounting information and to keep track of both continuously. Before the computer age, acquiring information was usually a major task, and often its value was not worth the effort. Getting the correct raw data is sometimes still elusive, but computer technology now has made it easy to calculate and present information in almost any form imaginable. It is time, or past time, to apply the benefits of the computer age to the budgeting process. Accounting and financial reporting needs are just not an excuse for the absence of required management information.

Fixed and Variable Cost Budgeting

Let us turn now to techniques for improving the budget format. The first is directed at the types of businesses that use direct and indirect expense and burden rates. It is usually explained, as it is here, in terms of a manufacturing business. However, a short example near the end of this section shows how it can be a useful thought process in other kinds of businesses.

Beyond those problems addressed earlier, another difficulty with the focus on overheads and burden rates is that a particular ratio fits only a small range of variables because of the fixed nature of some costs. The use of *gross margin* (sales minus fully burdened direct costs divided by sales) illustrates the point. Any factory includes in its burdens (overheads) a number of fixed costs (costs that do not vary with sales). Rent is an obvious example, but the salaries of the manufacturing engineers are another example, unless their number expands and contracts immediately and directly with variations in sales. Gross margin thus varies widely with sales level. If sales of any product decrease, direct costs will decrease but fixed costs will not. A given amount of fixed cost will have to be spread over a smaller direct cost base. Thus, gross margin of a particular product will decrease for a reason that has nothing to do with the profitability of that product. Similarly, an overhead rate can increase simply because sales, and therefore direct labor, do not materialize, which says nothing about how well the factory is being managed.

A better way to budget, manage, and measure is on the basis of fixed and variable costs, sometimes called "flexible budgeting."

Fixed costs are those that do not vary with *sales*. (There is no implication that fixed costs are fixed over *time*, or that they cannot be reduced. The test is whether a cost will be incurred if a particular sale is not made; if so, it is a fixed cost.) Costs classified as indirect are usually in the fixed category, while costs classified as direct are usually variable. Direct costs need not be variable, however; an example of fixed direct costs is time charges to a customer contract by the engineering department. If the engineers are not fired immediately when a sale does not materialize, they are really a fixed cost. Similarly, any indirect cost that is removed if a sale is lost is variable.

With fixed and variable cost budgeting, the profitability parameter of interest becomes the *contribution margin* (sales minus variable costs divided by sales) rather than gross margin. This is a better measure of profitability of a product line, because it considers only those costs directly associated with that product line. Its value is independent of the level of sales of the subject product, and also independent of sales of other products.

The process of preparing the budget numbers is also easier and more focused. Use of fixed and variable costs permits the basic categories of sales, margin, and fixed cost to be prepared almost separately. With overheads, burdens, and gross margins, all these parameters of interest change with different amounts of sales or indirect cost. On the other hand, if fixed costs are predicted, they can then be held constant as different sales levels are postulated; or, if sales vary widely enough to cause changes in fixed cost, cause and effect can be seen clearly.

As an example of flexible budgeting, consider a factory that sells products A, B, and C. For simplicity, assume that direct equals variable expense and indirect equals fixed expense. Also assume no G&A or other expense beyond a factory indirect expense of $2 million (i.e., gross margin dollars equal profit). Assume that the budget is $800,000 in sales of product A with $200,000 in direct expense, $1 million in sales of product B with $300,000 in direct expense, and $1.5 million in sales of product C with $500,000 in direct expense. In traditional budgeting, a simple single overhead rate would be indirect divided by direct expense (or $2,000,000/($200,000 + $300,000 + $500,000) = 200%). A traditional budget would be as follows (COS is cost of sales):

Product	Sales	*(Numbers in thousands of dollars)* Direct Expense	Overhead	COS	Profit
A	800	200	400	600	200
B	1,000	300	600	900	100
C	1,500	500	1,000	1,500	0
Total	3,300	1,000	2,000	3,000	300

A flexible budget carries only direct expense with the product and subtracts indirect expense from contribution margin to get profit. The same budget using flexible budgeting would be as follows (CM is contribution margin):

Product	Sales	*(Numbers in thousands of dollars)* Variable Expense	CM
A	800	200	600
B	1,000	300	700
C	1,500	500	1,000
Total CM			2,300
Fixed expense			2,000
Profit			300

Quite a different picture: The traditional method says that product C is not profitable (because its large relative sales make it carry half the indirect expense), while the flexible budget shows it contributing $1 million of profit.

Now assume that the budget is changed in the belief that 1,000 sales of product A can be achieved with the same percent contribution margin but with no increase in indirect expense. The increased product A sales add $50,000 in direct expense, so the overhead is now $2,000,000/$1,050,000 = 190% (rounded). The new traditional budget would be as follows:

		(Numbers in thousands of dollars)			
		Direct			
Product	Sales	Expense	Overhead	COS	Profit
A	1,000	250	476	726	274
B	1,000	300	571	871	129
C	1,500	500	953	1,453	47
Total	3,500	1,050	2,000	3,050	450

Nothing changed concerning product C, but it now shows a small profit. The new flexible budget would be:

			Variable	
	(Numbers in thousands of dollars)			
Product		Sales	Expense	CM
A		1,000	250	750
B		1,000	300	700
C		1,500	500	1,000
Total CM				2,450
Fixed expense				2,000
Profit				450

The flexible budget clearly relates the increased profit to its cause—increased sales of product A—while the traditional format obscures the cause by showing each product as more profitable. The flexible budget also allows management to focus on fixed expense, the break-even point, and the relative profitability of the different products.

As an example from a totally different arena, consider a business that sells personal services, such as a consulting company or law firm. If sales are predicted (i.e., pricing determined) by applying a markup to the salary of the employees who do the work, the business is using flexible budgeting, even though that term is probably not used. If the business determines prices by spreading fixed costs as a ratio of performing employee (i.e., direct) costs, that approach is comparable to traditional overhead/gross margin budgeting. The latter method would tell the personal services company to increase prices in a downturn, because the ratio of fixed to (smaller) direct costs would be higher. Such reasoning could make the company price itself out of its market.

The use of fixed and variable cost budgeting yields several benefits and advantages over traditional budgeting, including these:

• Product and service profitability are measured by contribution margin, rather than gross margin. The former is a direct measure, whereas the latter includes a number of elements not related to product profitability.

• The entire organization knows the fixed costs, i.e., what it costs to open the doors every morning, even if not a single sale is made.

• It makes evident to everyone whether the company is a high-fixed- or high-variable-cost business. The problems and strategies of the two are quite different.

• It lets the organization focus directly on the appropriateness of incremental pricing. Incremental pricing, meaning pricing that covers only direct costs, is correctly the bane of most accountants. Clearly, if every sale is incrementally priced, the business will lose money. However, if there is idle capacity, it may be beneficial to price a piece of new business incrementally. If no fixed expense needs to be added for this piece of business, the entire contribution margin will drop to the bottom line. To turn this around, many businesses confront situations in which they want a piece of new business that will have important long-term effects but for which they will have to lower their normal price. Fixed and variable cost budgeting and measurement will directly present the impact of the pricing decision. Further, if the organization is used to thinking in this way, the proper incremental reasoning will be almost automatic.

All that having been said, there is a major imperfection of fixed and variable cost budgeting. Fixed expense is not really "fixed." In most businesses, different product lines or different activities require different amounts of indirect expense. One product line may need more manufacturing engineering than another product line in a factory. A product in a retail business that requires heavy inventory demands more accounting resources than a product or service that does not. These factors must be kept in mind and analyzed to get a true picture of the profitability of different parts of the company. In other words, flexible budgeting is an improvement over traditional budgeting in relating variable activities to business outputs, but it does nothing for so-called fixed, or indirect, activities. The following sections show how to get closer to the goal of relating the cost of *every* activity to outputs.

Activity-Based Costing

Activity-based costing (ABC) is a relatively new technique that can theoretically relate every activity to business outputs. It thus has the potential for completing the job begun by flexible budgeting.

ABC is a cost management system that relates all work activity of a company to its output—i.e., products shipped and services performed—and ultimately to sales. One defines each work activity, identifies its cost drivers, and uses these drivers to assign costs to products shipped and the services performed. In concept, this is only an extension of traditional methods: If direct labor is truly the cost driver of all indirect factory expense, burdening direct labor with its proportion of indirect cost would indeed be part of an ABC system. Practically, however, the difference between ABC and traditional methods is huge, requiring extensive work and changes of thinking, but ABC can yield large management benefits.

The extensive work involved is mainly the definition of activities, as well as of inputs, outputs, and cost drivers. Consider just one element of the assembly of an electronic product: the stuffing (i.e., the insertion and soldering of components) of a printed circuit board that goes into that product. A complex printed circuit board designed as many such boards still are could involve automatic and manual insertion of components. The activities for just this one circuit board could include supplying material to each work station, setup of the automatic insertion machine, automatic insertion, manual insertion, soldering, and inspection.

Practical systems would include some summarization and combination of activities. However, for the total product, there might be a page of activities to describe what used to be one line (direct labor applied to the product) in traditional cost systems. Charges would then be accumulated by activity as well as by product or project. The change in thinking required by those involved is obvious.

The definition of activities is, however, a major task only at first, and the benefits of improved management information can be large. Typically, fixed or indirect expenses do not vary predominantly with the number of units produced, as implied by spreading most overhead cost on direct labor. But some expenses, such as machine setup, vary with the number of "batches"—i.e., number of different types of circuit boards put through the assembly facility. Others, such as assembly process design, vary with the number of products. Still others, related to administration or maintenance of the facility, are essentially independent of the level of factory activity. ABC allows development of cost drivers related to "units," "batches," "products," "administration," and "facility." Thus ABC gives managers a better picture of the real profitability of different products, and also shows them where to look for improvement in managing the factory.

Partial Implementation of ABC

Full implementation of ABC requires totally recasting the budget and management reporting into an activity-based structure that directly relates business outputs to all contributing activities. It is a huge step for most companies. First, in ABC, people are asked to think in a very different way, and they will be managed and measured on that new way. Both inborn resistance to change and unfamiliarity with the new concept will operate. Also, participants will be suspicious that the whole process is just another cost-cutting exercise. Second, it can be difficult to identify cost drivers with satisfying precision. If that cannot be done, the result will be that copious amounts of work will have been done, only to replace one arbitrary system with a new system just as arbitrary. Third, with apologies and hopes for success to the apostles of ABC, I believe that it is fair to say that ABC is still in the pioneering stage, and pioneers often get arrows in their backs.

Because of the difficulties, the optimum application of ABC for many companies will be *partial* implementation. The budgeting need is to relate activities to business outputs. Traditional methods and flexible budgeting particularly fail in relating *indirect* activities to outputs. The principles of ABC can be used to remedy that failing without full implementation.

However, the intent is not to discourage any company from full implementation of ABC. It is, after all, theoretically the ideal technique to ensure that the budgeting format satisfies the "most useful information for management" objective. ABC is a popular topic in consulting circles these days, and good outside help in fully implementing ABC is available if desired. The large accounting firms offer this as part of their consulting practice.*

The recommendation is partial implementation of ABC, using it for all indirect activities (including G&A and corporate expense, which are covered separately in following sections). The goal is to define all activities, identify the main things that drive their costs, and budget and charge the activities ultimately to products according to the relationships with the most prominent cost drivers. The considerations and benefits of this partial implementation and the procedure for accomplishing it are discussed in succeeding paragraphs.

Considerations

Most of the considerations involved in partially implementing ABC can be seen in a single example, a company's payroll func-

---

*For further information on the subject, see *Activity Accounting* by James A. Brimson (New York: John Wiley & Sons, 1991).

tion. Ask the question, "Why does this particular company need seven payroll clerks? Why not ten—or five?" The activities of a typical payroll function include reviewing and entering time records, reviewing payroll data prepared by the computer, entering changes in salaries and benefits, correcting errors, making adjustments, and handling inquiries. At intervals, changes must be made in the system to accommodate changes in various tax regulations. Intuitively, the principal cost driver of the payroll function's total work load is the number of people on the payroll. However, in most cases drivers that are just as strong or stronger include the number of errors, the number of adjustments that must be made, and special factors such as how many states the employees work in (which dictates how many state tax schemes must be accommodated).

Typically, the analyst of payroll cost drivers will find that the work load is very inelastic; if seven payroll clerks can handle a 2,000-person payroll, three might be required for 200 employees, and the seven might be able to handle growth to 3,000. In other words, there seems to be a core work load almost independent of variation in any of the drivers; addition or subtraction of an entire product line will probably not change payroll costs much one way or the other. So the results for payroll function costs might not be very satisfying. However, one might conclude that the main cost drivers are the number of people on the payroll (errors and adjustments are probably proportional to this) plus the number of states in which there are employees.

Even though results in the payroll example do not yield strong, linear cost drivers, the fact that the work load is constant over a wide range of business activity is useful information. It says that payroll cost can be arbitrarily allocated without much loss of information. Also, the payroll function is a relatively small cost anyway, probably beyond the point of diminishing returns. (Payroll's universality, not its importance, recommended it as an example.) Still, consider a bank operating in one state that decides to open loan offices in ten new states. If the added cost of administration of all the different state taxes, including payroll, is spread over the entire business, the new product line will look more profitable than it really is. Management has better information on which to evaluate the new business if that added state-related administrative cost is charged against it.

The payroll example illustrates just about all aspects of introducing ABC into a traditional environment. The people will be uneasy that their function is being analyzed; they will not understand it initially and think that some of their jobs are in jeopardy. For some functions, the correlation of activity with output will be elusive. However, such "negative" information is also useful, and the principle of diminishing returns applies: Most of the gain comes from relating only the most important activities to outputs. Finally, any information about any activity can improve management's knowledge of the relative profitability of all of its activities.

Benefits

The first benefit of partial implementation of ABC is a fundamental one: It allows indirect activities to be rationally related to business outputs. Second, it is a prime example of incremental gain for incremental effort; it lends itself to experimentation. Every single conclusion about an activity cost driver gives management more useful information about relative profitability. (An ABC element can be inserted into a traditional budget; there is even value if the budget is not changed and the ABC results are only used separately for relative profitability analysis.)

Third, the initial resistance and skepticism of the organization should develop into support if the process is handled well. Managers want to know what drives their costs and they already work hard at determining that. Any process that helps them do this, and then realistically applies the results to their budgeting and measurement, will ultimately be welcome. Fourth, if the company needs to cut costs, an ABC analysis is perhaps the most intelligent way to approach that problem.

Fifth, ABC facilitates development of action plans and selection of the most fruitful areas for action. Action plans must address activities. If an organization already thinks and budgets in terms of activities, the step to good action planning is a smaller one. With traditional budgeting, a problem statement in an insurance company might be that sales costs are too high, a problem statement requiring further definition before action can be planned. With ABC, the original statement of the same problem might be, "Policy proposal costs are too high." This problem can be addressed with no further definition.

Finally, some cost drivers are not obscure but yield their identities quickly to analysis, leading to early benefits. Some of these seem obvious, but only after the analysis is done. A study of the work load of a purchasing function found that the most prominent cost driver was simply the number of purchase orders, which also drove some data-processing and accounting costs. Company control procedures and business practices resulted in this purchasing function being inundated with a large number of very small purchase orders. As a result of the study, the company was able to institute a simpler procedure for small purchases that made a considerable impact on the purchasing function's work load and cost.

Implementation Procedure

Even partial implementation of activity-based costing is a major task, but it can be made easier. ABC should be announced as an experiment and begun in only two or three functions, chosen for both their ease of analysis and resident analytical ability. It must not be perceived as a cost-cutting exercise; do not say, "Why do you need ten people to do this?" Rather, say "What determines that you need ten people to do this, rather than fifteen or five?" The analysis should be done by the function in question, with help and direction. As tentative conclusions are developed, they should be checked against history. If in the past that particular function employed considerably different resources, why was that? Direction and assistance will be needed if the concept is unfamiliar.

After the function to be analyzed is identified, the first step is to define activities and their inputs and outputs. Typical activities of a regional sales office are telephone contacts and cold calls on potential customers, sales presentations of products and services, preparation of proposals, negotiation of orders, continuing customer relations, and representing the company in the region. Every function has another category, perhaps called "administration," that includes the various managerial and administrative activities.

The next step is to assign the function's costs to the different activities. Some will be obvious, some will require considerable analysis, and some small ones should probably be arbitrarily allocated.

With the function's cost by activity in hand, the cost drivers of the different activities must be determined. The search is for the strongest relationships to inputs or outputs, suitable as a basis for charging the costs of the function. In the earlier purchasing example, the cost driver selected was the number of purchase orders; in a different situation, the number of engineering change notices could be a major driver of purchasing costs, requiring frequent changes and expediting of purchase orders. The main cost driver of a regional sales office could vary greatly over time with the type and maturity of products or services sold, but it would be related to the nature of those products or services, along with orders required and customer characteristics.

When conclusions about cost driver relationships have been reached, they must be applied to the budget. In the purchasing example, the costs of the purchasing function would be removed from the overhead pool in which they reside. These costs would then be assigned to products, services, or to support organizations in proportion to the number of purchase orders they generate, and the managers responsible for them would have to budget the expected number and cost of those purchase orders.

The recommendation is to do this as a fixed charge per purchase order. If purchasing costs are allocated as a ratio of purchase orders to purchasing function cost, the company is right back in the ratio problem again: A product line's cost varies inversely to the company's total number of purchase orders (the base on which they are spread), which again may have nothing to do with that product line's requirements. With a fixed charge, there will be a positive or negative variance or residual, which must be put in an overhead pool, arbitrarily allocated, or held separately (again, perfection is not achieved). This gives the side benefit of direct visibility into the cost control activities of the purchasing manager; he or she should get the credit if a given amount of work is accomplished with lower cost, and this will be apparent.

Assignment of G&A and Corporate Expense

General and administrative (G&A) expense is a standard cost category used by most companies to account for overall management and support costs and for those costs that do not directly relate to a product or service. The office of the head of the business (the president or division general manager), accounting, treasury, human resources, and management information systems are all typical G&A expenses. G&A expense is sometimes held and reported separately or allocated to products, services, or related organizations on an arbitrary basis, as are sales or cost of sales.

Most multidivisional companies have a category of expense called something like "corporate," which includes the general expenses of running the overall company. Examples are the president's salary, investor relations activities, and, in smaller companies, functions centralized at the corporate level, such as human resources. Centralized functions are usually installed to get the benefits of minimum cost and professionalism.

The budgeting problem for G&A and corporate expense is the same. The common practice of holding them separately or allocating them arbitrarily does not supply information regarding profitability and benefits and consequences of action.

The work of G&A organizations and corporate staffs consists of *activities*, just like that of any other business unit. Some of these activities are disproportionately related to, or caused by, a particular product or division. An example is a company with separate profit centers for products and for the maintenance service of those products. The manufacturing profit center will probably use more accounting resources per dollar of sales, because cost and inventory accounting for manufacturing is more complex than for service. If G&A and corporate expense are arbitrarily allocated, based on something like cost of sales, these cost/output relationships are obscured.

The budgeting format needed for G&A and corporate expense is the same as that stated throughout this chapter: The activities must be related to business outputs if management is to obtain the most useful information possible.

The first step in intelligently assigning G&A and corporate expense is to determine which are "true" G&A and corporate costs and which are "assignable." "True" costs are those that exist just because the company exists, independent of any particular product or division, and do not vary with product or divisional sales or profit. "Assignable" costs are those that directly relate to a product or division and vary with the needs of that particular product or division.

All costs associated with the company's president and his or her office are examples of true G&A or corporate expense. In multidivisional companies, some costs are incurred simply because there is a corporate structure above the divisions (businesses): acquisition and divestiture planning (unless instigated by one of the divisions), company financial and business planning, and community relations at a headquarters location separate from any of the divisions. If the profitability of a product or a division is being evaluated or compared with competitors', it is not realistic to include a portion of those "corporate structure" charges in product or division expense. Other examples of true G&A and corporate expense include:

- Staff organizations whose prime mission is coordination or audit (as opposed to those that assist divisions and product lines with particular expertise).
- Corporate expense that is simply the cost of being a public company: various legal costs, public financial reporting, investor relations, transfer agent costs, etc.
- "Historical" corporate costs such as settlement costs in an old dispute involving a discontinued business, or costs to correct an old environmental problem that cannot be ascribed to a current operation.
- "Cultural" G&A or corporate costs in a private company, e.g., various perquisites given by the owner to himself or herself.

In short, there are various categories of true G&A and corporate costs that should not be assigned to products or divisions, because they are independent of product or division activity. In budgeting, it is recommended that they be held separately and not allocated so as not to distort product or division profitability. However, the disadvantage is that some operating people might be satisfied with too small a profit; they might "forget" that the corporate costs are real and must be covered by sales and margin. If the latter is the primary concern, the true G&A and corporate costs should be allocated on an arbitrary basis, but should be held out of evaluation and measurement of the divisions.

After true G&A and corporate costs are identified and removed, the assignable costs should be charged on the basis of activities to the product or division to which they relate. Some activities will be obvious, and costs can be accumulated as a project and charged directly to the appropriate product or division: computer programming, facilities alteration, or a project done by a research laboratory. For the service areas that are not obvious, the best method again is activity-based costing.

Special Factors Regarding G&A and Corporate Expense

There are special factors concerning G&A and corporate expense that extend beyond the realm of budgeting but are important because they are part of the objective of providing the information most useful to management. Analyzing these special factors is also useful as a reasonableness check in budgeting.

The following discussion treats a multidivision company for simplicity and for direct applicability. However, it could be equally applicable to a single business if *product line* is substituted for "division" and *G&A* is substituted for "corporate" expense.

These special factors relate to the problem that the proper way to budget corporate charges, described above, may not give the right information for evaluating a division for prospective sale or discontinuation. The right budgeting question is, "How should we charge the assignable corporate costs that we will incur?" The right questions for sale or discontinuation of a division are (1) What support costs would the division need to add to operate as a completely stand-alone business? and (2) What corporate costs would be eliminated if the division were gone from the company?

It is recommended that analysis of these two questions be done periodically, in conjunction with budgeting, for the useful information this will supply, even if no sales or discontinuations are contemplated.

Consider the implications of the two questions. First, the stand-alone support costs for a division should be higher than the budgeted assignable corporate costs charged to it. If not, the company is not getting the benefits of cost minimization from centralization. Second, the amount of cost reduction that would accompany discontinuation or sale of a division should be less than this assignable charge of corporate costs, again because some cost minimization and efficiency should be attained by centralizing various functions.

Relative to budgeting, analyzing these questions will yield conclusions about whether the level of assignable corporate costs is reasonable. There are generally operating advantages in decentralizing every possible function, because these "support" functions then become more customer-conscious and customer-driven. The reason for centralizing functions is to get the benefits of cost minimization and professionalism. If the cost relationships are not as they should be, the benefit of cost minimization is not being achieved. This can provide the motivation for a useful study of how that centralized function should really be performed.

Beyond budgeting, the other value of analyzing these questions is the better picture of profitability that results. For example, companies sometimes find that one or two divisions require practically all the assignable corporate costs by themselves. What does that tell the president of the company? Assume a company with Divisions A, B, and C, and assume that A itself requires 90 percent of assignable corporate cost. That is, if both B and C were eliminated, only 10 percent of the cost would be saved. This tells the president, first, that he is almost getting a free ride with divisions B and C; as long as A is in business, B and C are probably desirable even if they do not make much profit. Second, it tells him that A is not as profitable as he probably thought it was, because it requires so much corporate support. Third, if he sells A he would be in for a shock, because B and C would no longer get the free ride and the possible reduction in corporate expense would be smaller than expected. The answer to these questions supplies a more informed basis for concentration decisions and for the employment and deployment of resources.

Realism vs. Complexity

Fixed and variable cost budgeting, partial or full activity-based costing, and activity-based assignment of corporate charges should be thought of as candidate techniques. While each or all should be useful, each company must find the unique solution that fits it best in substance and style and best attacks the problems it faces.

In developing a particular solution, a company must balance realism and complexity. There must be enough detail so that activities are realistically portrayed; otherwise the information is not as useful as it could be. But in this information age, it is possible to be so overwhelmed with the volume of available data that little information is obtained from it. The expansion of the budget format must stop before the resulting complexity negates the benefits being sought.

Fixed and variable cost budgeting is actually a simplifying step, rather than a complicator. It allows managers to obtain a given level of understanding with fewer numbers and fewer calculations. Activity-based costing, however, is the opposite. ABC replaces, for example, a single "corporate charge" number with many numbers related to many cost drivers. The ideal would be to relate every cost through cost drivers to business output. However, as ABC analysis expands to cover every activity in a company, there is clearly a point of diminishing returns.

Care must be taken, however, to distinguish between important and unimportant detail. Managers at every level should get whatever detail they need to realistically manage the important items for which they are responsible. The crucial items may well change over time; there is nothing wrong with changing the format when that occurs. Otherwise, however, detail should be avoided, because unimportant detail has the potential for making management focus on unimportant things. Also, unimportant detail may not be worth the effort needed to gather and present it.

Conclusion

The most useful information for management is that which best portrays the benefits and consequences of its activities and actions. What that information is must be addressed in selecting the budgeting format because the periodic reports used to manage the business should be in the same format as the budget. To provide the most useful information for management, the budget format must (1) emphasize profit and cash flow directly, (2) focus management's attention on total costs, rather than on burden rates and ratios, and (3) relate business outputs to *activities*.

Traditional methods often obscure rather than clarify these things. Most burden rates and ratios used in these methods erroneously (1) assign costs based on a gross parameter that is not the driver of those costs and (2) apply expense or sales changes in one product to the profitability of another.

A step in the right direction is to base the budget format on flexible budgeting, i.e., on fixed and variable costs. This assigns only the variable costs associated with a product to that product. Fixed costs, those that do not vary with sales are held separately. Flexible budgeting yields a number of advantages over traditional methods: a direct measure of product profitability, knowledge of the fixed costs of the business, information concerning whether the company is a high-fixed- or high-variable-cost business, and a focus on the appropriateness of incremental pricing.

The major imperfection of flexible budgeting is that it does not assign fixed cost to products or services. There is nothing fundamental about the distinction between direct and indirect costs. Indeed, as businesses of all kinds implement more automation, indirect costs become proportionally larger and more variable.

Activity-based costing is a mechanism that can potentially relate all costs directly to the products or services that cause them. It is a cost management system that relates all work activity of a company to its outputs. The cost drivers of each activity are defined and used to assign costs to products shipped and services rendered. Implementing ABC can be a major challenge, because people are asked to think in a very different way and because it can be difficult to identify the cost drivers with satisfying precision. For these reasons, partial implementation of ABC—for all indirect costs—will be the best solution for many companies. Even imperfect or partial steps toward ABC will give a company a better understanding of the profitability of different products and services.

Assignment of general and administrative and corporate costs to divisions, products, and services has some special problems. However, assigning such costs on an activity basis, rather than in accordance with sales or cost of sales, not only makes budgeting more valuable but also can be a major tool in strategic analysis.

An instructive example of the progression of thinking about profitability is a contract manufacturing business with which I became associated some years ago. The business of contract manufacturing is to manufacture customers' products. The customers design and specify the products and later sell them; the contract manufacturer supplies the service of making those products. At the beginning I was told, "We want jobs with heavy direct labor content." That sounded like a strange goal, but what was really meant was that this business could get a much higher markup on direct labor than it could on material, its other major cost. Therefore, it was properly, up to a point, seeking high-markup jobs. However, it was missing the point that not all high-direct-markup jobs were equal. In fact, the highest-markup job (i.e., apparently the most profitable) was complex and involved a number of different products; analysis showed that this job was by far the biggest user of indirect resources in that business. When total costs, direct and indirect, were taken into account, it turned out that the most profitable type of job was one in which hundreds of one product were banged out every month, even though the labor content and contribution margin were small. Both sales and profitability of that business grew rapidly as the focus was changed to the latter type of work.

FUNCTIONAL MANAGERS: SURMOUNTING A POOR BUDGETING PROCESS

The functional manager must submit and discuss his or her budget in terms of the format dictated by the division or company. If the budgeting process is poor, chances are that this format will not be very useful. To be able to manage effectively, he or she must get the most useful information possible.

The functional manager should rigorously analyze activities, inputs, and outputs; understanding them is required to do the job, in any event. From this analysis, he or she can decide which information and parameters are most useful. The functional manager should then develop a private budget form in those terms, put it on a personal computer spreadsheet, and track it throughout the year. If the climate is right, he or she should share both the budget and the tracking with his or her superior. Some of the information may not be readily available in the company's system. A trade-off will have to be made between the value of some information and the difficulty in getting it. However, some improvements will undoubtedly be both worth doing and easy to do.

Again, a purchasing manager in manufacturing is a good example. Assume that the company's budgeting format and cost system assign all functional costs to material overhead, and that the material bought is charged to direct material, by project. Assume that top management keeps close tabs on the material overhead rate, so the purchasing manager must pay attention to the relation of the function's costs to the material bought. However, these numbers do not help him manage. The purchasing manager's concerns for next year are (1) to minimize the cost of direct material and (2) to learn what specific products, types of products, and organization of projects make the purchasing function cost more or less. The purchasing manager has developed new processes and procedures to address the former (preferably as a result of gap analysis; see Chapter 11). Regarding the latter, the manager is in the data-gathering stage but hopes eventually to influence company superiors toward more efficient product types and project structures.

In this example, it is relatively easy for the purchasing manager to get more useful information to help minimize the cost of direct material. The system already gives direct material cost by project. The manager can set up goals and status quo numbers for material costs on each project and can also track the processes and procedures used on each project. The manager will then be able to measure results against goals and to measure the effectiveness of the various new processes and procedures that have been instituted.

For the second concern, discovering how different products and project formats affect purchasing function costs, the purchasing manager can implement private time recording. Although the system does not require it, the manager can have all purchasing personnel fill out weekly time sheets by project, for purchasing department use only. By later categorizing products and projects according to relevant characteristics (production amount, complexity, labor versus material content, procedures relative to production release and bills of material, etc.), the manager can gather the desired data of purchasing effort versus product and project types. A good manager will have involved his or her employees and boss in this entire activity.

This example shows how comparatively minor actions relative to useful information format can increase a functional manager's ability to do a better job. One may argue that the example treats management in general, rather than budgeting. The answer is that budgeting *is* part of management, and the budgeting process is the natural time and place to define the most useful information. The management information format is dictated by the budget format. If the latter is good, the former will be good. If the budget format is not good, the management information will never be what is needed.

The functional manager must pay close attention to the company's budget format; it contains the things that top management tracks. If burden rations are prominent, he or she must be sensitive to the ratios. However, the manager should keep his or her superior informed of the private budget form and explain problems and good results in those terms whenever possible. The problem comes when the two budget forms seem to contradict each other, i.e., when a functional manager's proposed action would reduce total cost but increase the overhead rate. In this case the manager has to sell the action, and the private budget form is one of the bases for the sale. The manager is asking, in effect, for permission to miss one budgeted number in return for a greater positive effect on other company numbers. This is a fairly common management discussion; if competent and objective, the functional manager will win more of these than he or she will lose.

10

Developing the Content: The Best Numbers

A large part of getting the best numbers into the budget lies in doing all the preparation right. This book advocates "thinking it through before crunching the numbers." However, putting the numbers in the budget, after all, is the payoff of the budgeting process. If not done well, the whole process goes for naught.

Therefore, after the best parameters for the budget format are selected, the next problem is to select the best numbers to put into that format. The budget deals with the unknown future, and the numbers that express expected performance for the following year are necessarily estimates. The requirement is to make these numerical entries the most probable and meaningful they can be.

There are only three sources of budgeting estimates: data, trends, and models. *Data* in this sense means specific information about future events; sales backlog to be shipped in the coming year is an example, as is a costed bill of material for a product. *Trends* are the general directions that particular parameters have been moving; extrapolating trends into the future is the way they are used in budgeting. If a particular product had sales of 40, 80, and 120 units, respectively, in the last three years, the trend would say that 160 units would be sold next year. *Models* (strictly, mathematical models) are equations or sets of equations that describe the relationships among parameters and predict results for given values of related parameters. The equation

$$Profit = Sales - Expense$$

is a model, although obviously too simple to be of much value in a budget. Models may be implicit. Assume that a sales manager says, "There are 1,000 customers for this product line, and they each replace their equipment every five years, so I believe there will be 200 orders next year." He has built this implicit model in his mind, even if he has never written down the equation:

$$\text{Orders} = 20\% \times \text{Market}$$

Even for a new activity, with no data or trends, in which the estimate of the next year's performance seems to come out of the air, an implicit model is being used for that judgment.

The problem that causes deterioration in the value of the numerical content of budgets is mainly misuse of data, trends, or models. A typical problem is stretching data beyond the time they are meaningful. Some people labor to put specific customer names and dates on orders expected to be received in the fourth quarter of the next year by using data about current prospects. If the order cycle is six months, one cannot know the specific identity of customers who will place orders a year from now. It would undoubtedly be more accurate to use trends or a model involving known market size, prospects, sales calls, etc., to estimate fourth-quarter orders. Similarly, in that same company, if the financial people develop the cash flow budget based on such specific orders, material purchase time, receivables time, etc., that will undoubtedly be much work for little value. The projected result will be in great detail but extremely unlikely to happen. Much more useful would be a cash flow budget based on a cash flow model, rather than predictions about specific transactions a year away.

The most common problem regarding trends results from blindly following them. The only certainty about the future is that things will change. Just because a clear trend has been established does not mean that it will continue. Whether it does or not will depend on both changes in the outside environmental factors (OEFs) and internal changes that management makes. If widgets have been assembled by the company for two years and management has not changed the process, the cost of assembling a widget in the coming year is very predictable. However, one can never say that an orders trend will continue without examining market factors, competition's actions, the general economy, etc.

The opposite problem also occurs: ignoring trends. The manager who predicts a doubling of sales that have been flat for three years obviously has some explaining to do.

The most common problems with models are that they are not used enough and are used incorrectly. Some businesses use models extensively and are very fluent in their language. In others managers have never been formally introduced to the subject and are not comfortable with it. Such businesses must educate their managers in proper use of mathematical models for budgeting and analysis. If not, their budgets will continue to suffer from use of outdated data and overreliance on trends. Models do not have to be complicated to be useful in budgeting; a later section of this chapter explains valuable modeling that anyone can do.

Predicting Sales

The critical judgments—and the most difficult—in developing the numerical content of the budget are the amount of business that will be achieved (i.e., orders, sales units) and at what price (i.e., sales prices, margins). Future sales are always uncertain. (Some types of businesses use the term *revenue* rather than *sales*; they have the same meaning here.)

There is a fundamental difference in the orders/sales forecasting problem among different types of businesses. In Chapter 8, "hockey" businesses and "basketball" businesses were discussed. The former involve few sales, but they are for large dollar amounts; the latter depend on a large volume of small sales. In the computer business, a supercomputer manufacturer is an example of the former, while a personal computer maker is an example of the latter. Most retailing businesses are "basketball" businesses, although the new car sales department of a luxury car dealership is probably a "hockey" business. Many companies include both types of businesses; maintenance service in the new car dealership and parts sales by the supercomputer manufacturer are "basketball" businesses. The type of business in this sense is defined by orders, rather than sales. A bottle manufacturer may sell millions of bottles in a year, but if it depends on only ten customers to buy all its bottles, it is clearly in the "hockey" category.

If a business relies on a few large sales, each order is quite important, and the presence or absence of one particular order can make or break a year. In that case, little value can be obtained from probability, statistics, or trends, whereas the business with many small sales relies on them.

Another pertinent dividing line is whether or not orders are important to the business. An order is an agreement to buy something at a specified future time and price and implies that work must be done before delivery. Orders are a most meaningful and important concept for many manufacturing and service businesses, while they mean nothing for most retail stores, where people come through the door and pay cash. Where orders are meaningful, "backlog," meaning orders received but not yet delivered (or "sold"), is an important budgeting and management parameter. On the other hand, "backlog" has no meaning for a grocery store.

Thus, for discussion of the crucial task of predicting sales, distinctions among different generic types of businesses must be kept in mind: those with few-but-large sales, those with many-but-small sales, and whether orders is a meaningful concept.

Data, Trends, and Models

For the "hockey" business, where the presence or absence of just one or a few sales, and their timing, can make or break a year, the challenge of budgeting sales is formidable. For the business in which orders are meaningful, the first step in forecasting sales and margins is to spread the backlog. This is a data-gathering step and should be quite accurate and reliable. Then the hard part begins: forecasting new orders and sales.

Which orders estimates should come from data and which from trends or models? The key is the minimum time ordinarily involved from identifying a prospect until closing the order. Whatever amount of this time runs into the next year must be covered by data for identified potential customers already in the order cycle. If it ordinarily takes at least eight months from first contact to closing the order, and the budget is being prepared in early November, the first six months of the next year must be budgeted from data on known prospects. In other words, in November all the possible prospects are known for orders before July of the following year. Neither model nor trend nor anything else can help in getting other orders before July. Some such prospects in the order cycle will take longer than the minimum time, and they should also be entered into the budget as specific data.

Beyond such confident data points, modeling should be used, rather than data. The reasons for not using data beyond the order cycle time are that (1) such projections are usually wrong and (2) they imply definitive knowledge that does not exist. Consider a budget that contains an order for $1 million from the Ajax Company next November, a year from budget preparation. That budget entry identifies three important facts: customer name, order amount, and order timing. It is unlikely that things will happen just that way, but the specificity implies confidence. The organization will focus on the Ajax Company order long after the prospect has disappeared and, one hopes, has been replaced by other, better prospects. The budget submitter will be called on frequently to explain the status of the Ajax order and what went wrong. His or her credibility will suffer. It would be much better if that submitter said, "My best judgment is that we can achieve x dollars of orders in the fourth quarter next year, of the y types of products, from the z list of potential customers, but I have no way of being more specific than that." This is the truth, and it puts the whole organization on the same page, misleading no one. It points the sales force at a target market for target products, tells the factory the range of work it should expect, and tells the treasurer roughly what cash will be needed for inventory and receivables.

The above statement "My best judgment . . ." comes from a model, or at least from implicitly modeling-type thinking, plus possibly trends that have been studied and are expected to continue. It involves reasoning through a set of mathematical relationships to a result.

For the few-but-large-sales businesses in which orders are not meaningful, models have to be the actual starting point of the reasoning. This type of business has no way to specifically identify customers and so cannot make the mistake of stretching orders prospect data beyond reliability. The luxury new car sales manager neither knows nor cares whether Mr. Green will buy a car; he or she deals in such parameters as advertising, sales promotion discounts, showroom traffic, and the local economy.

Orders and Sales Drivers

Models for predicting orders or sales are unique to each type of business, and almost to each individual business. However, the general orders/sales drivers from which the unique models come can be identified.

The first is the relevant market: its overall size, how many will buy in a year, seasonal tendencies, and the like. The supercomputer maker probably knows its total market specifically, including the actual names of all the laboratories, agencies, and businesses that are potential supercomputer users. The luxury new car dealer knows his or her market in terms of statistics: the number of people in the trading area with annual incomes exceeding a given amount, for example. Each company has particular market parameters within the market that are of direct interest. For a third-party computer maintenance company, an important orders model parameter is the number of companies in the potential market that will decide on a subcontracting policy and the number that will decide to stop subcontracting. For the business that sells millions of bottles to ten customers, the key concern is probably to identify the other prospects with the highest potential, as well as hold on to each of the ten current customers.

For some businesses, the potential market is so large it is not an issue. This is usually true for radically new products, such as television sets in 1950. At that time every household was a potential customer, but the pertinent parameter was how fast that huge potential market could be penetrated. On the other hand, for businesses in small markets, and market share leaders in any market, a primary concern has to be what is happening to the size of the market.

Another orders/sales driver is the state of the relevant economy. For the supercomputer maker, the size of the research and development portion of the defense budget is probably more pertinent than the state of the general economy, although the entire world economy may be pertinent to such a business. The new car dealer, on the other hand, is primarily concerned only with the local economy. For example, the recent relocation of the headquarters of a major corporation to the immediate area may have a salutary effect on luxury car sales.

A third general orders and sales driver is the actions of competitors. These include new products, price changes, entries and exits, and the like. This is probably the most important driver but the one that usually gets slighted in the budgeting process. We have all seen orders budgets in which competitor actions or prospective actions were ignored.

Competitors' expected *reactions* to company actions must also be considered. A phenomenon seen repeatedly concerns the situation where Company A and Company B divide a small market 50/50 or 40/60. Both are making comfortable profits, but then a hotshot in Company A decides that he can grow faster by taking away half of Company B's business by aggressive selling, lower prices, and faster deliveries. What Company A forgets is that Company B will react, with the same aggressive selling, lower prices, and faster deliveries. The usual result is that, after much turmoil, A and B settle back to their 50/50 or 40/60 split, but each of them is now making less profit. Competitors' reactions to any move must be considered, and the move should not be undertaken unless the company is convinced that it can develop an advantage that will last a long time.

Another driver is the maturity of the products and services the business offers. Sales of new products are much more difficult to predict than those of mature products.

A fifth general orders/sales driver is the company's sales and marketing organizations. For the "orders meaningful" type of business, this is primarily the sales force: its size, coverage, efficiency, and effectiveness. For the "orders not meaningful" category, this driver is primarily the marketing activity: the amount and effectiveness of advertising, the design of the product versus the competition's, sales promotion, and the like. In the few-but-large-sales business where orders are meaningful, a direct correlation between a salesperson's activity and sales is impossible, but there is clearly a relationship.

Last but not least, capacity is a sales driver; orders will not become sales unless the desired product or service can be delivered. Capacity here should be viewed in the broad sense to include skill and capacity as well as time and amount of resources.

Note that, of the six generalized order and sales drivers, only the last three—maturity of products, sales/marketing, and capacity—are within the company's control. The other three are uncontrollable outside environmental factors and are candidates for important budgeting assumptions (discussed in Chapter 8). As noted in Chapter 8, it is appropriate for top management and the board of directors to limit the number of orders OEFs they accept, expecting the organization to overcome some uncontrollable outside environmental changes. This does not change the thought process, however: It is necessary to study the expected outside environment and make assumptions about it before predicting orders and sales. Thus, one starting point for budgeting orders and sales is the assumptions process explained in Chapter 8.

Generating the Numbers

To summarize, for the "orders meaningful" business, the actual process to generate sales numbers for the budget starts with backlog, spreading it appropriately across the budget year. Next, the specific likely prospects already in the orders cycle (i.e., the pertinent *data*) are inserted. The expected behavior of OEFs is then taken from the assumptions process. The other inputs are management concerns: new products or services, discontinuation of products or services, type and size of marketing expense, and size and effectiveness of the sales force. There is no magic formula for putting these together for budget numbers; it is no more or less than the knowledge, experience, and good judgment for which management gets paid.

For the "orders not meaningful" business, the first two steps above do not apply. The same types of sales drivers exist, but the process should start with models, trends, and the expected behavior of the important OEFs. The most important drivers in this case tend to be demographics, products and prices relative to competition, the state of the economy, and the market position and reputation of the company and its products relative to the competition.

As a example of an orders-meaningful business, consider how the Mature division of the fictitious QRS Company (Chapters 2 and 3) should develop its orders and sales budgets. Mature, remember, is a declining business making and selling special purpose instrumentation computers, which are slowly but surely being replaced by general purpose computers. The corporate decision has been made to run out the business, making it as profitable and long-lasting as possible but not investing in it. The sales manager should spread his backlog and his likely orders prospects and then go through the following trend- and modeling-type thinking:

- The market size is known: 2,000 industrial and government laboratories worldwide. Mature has equipment in 1,000 of them.

- New laboratories take more than a year to complete, so it is also known that 80 new laboratories will begin operation next year, mostly in Eastern Asia.

- The conversion to general purpose computers is a major undertaking for these laboratories, requiring greatly different software and procedures. However, once a laboratory has converted, it is practically impossible for Mature to sell them anything. Most new laboratories will opt for general purpose computers.

- Of the 2,000 laboratories, 500 have already converted to general purpose computers. That trend is accelerating. Reasoning from the trend and specifics that he knows, the sales manager concludes that another 50 will convert during the coming year, and 25 will be Mature customers.

- Mature has two competitors for the specialized computers. It is difficult to dislodge a competitor, because of the extensive changes required in software and procedures.

- The laboratories in the past have made major purchases every five years, spread fairly uniformly, and smaller purchases every year. The sales manager stays familiar with the markets of his customers and believes that their business will accelerate next year to the point that 25 percent of them will make major purchases.

- There has typically been a seasonal factor because the purchase of instrumentation has seldom been time-critical to the customers, and capital budget money is released to Mature's customers late in the year. The seasonal factor usually results in 70 percent of annual orders being received in the second half of the year. The time from order to shipment is one month.

The sales manager decides to put no effort toward the 1,000 customers held by competitors, believing that they would change only to general purpose computers, not to Mature products. The major decision is the amount of effort to expend to sell the 80 new laboratories, given the expectation that most will opt for general purpose computers. Orders from new laboratories will be quite large, if successful. He concludes that he will challenge his sales force to sell 10 percent of the new laboratories; he is encouraged because he already has a strong indication of an order from one of them.

Whether he writes it down or not, the Mature sales manager has built a model for the orders he expects. After 25 defections to general purpose computers, he will have 975 customers. He expects large orders (call each $large) from 25 percent of them plus small orders ($small) from the rest. He expects to get total laboratory orders ($new) from 8 new laboratories (10 percent of the 80 known new laboratories). Thus:

$$
\begin{array}{lll}
\text{Orders} = 25\% \times 975 \times (\$large) & \text{(current customers)} \\
+ 75\% \times 975 \times (\$small) & \text{(current customers)} \\
+ 8 \times (\$new) & \text{(new laboratories)}
\end{array}
$$

He should then go back and compare this total with the entries already made from data on specific prospects, plus the expected output of the sales force, as a reasonableness check. He also should check the reasonableness of this total against his knowledge of customers' status and plans and Mature's position with them. That is, he should check the results of his model against his "hard" and "soft" data. He then should incorporate the seasonality factor of 70 percent of orders in the second half of the year. Finally, he should generate his sales budget from the orders by factoring in the one-month shipment time.

The few-but-large-sales business for which orders are meaningful should budget by quarter rather than by month. When each order is important, predicting them for specific months implies more information than can be available. (A typical problem with good salespeople is that they are reliable at forecasting *who* will buy, but too optimistic concerning *when* they will buy. Major purchases can easily take longer than one expects.) A useful management tool is then to prepare quarterly plans in the month preceding the applicable quarter, which detail and match either the budget or evolving reality by months. There should be reliable *data* with which to plan July–September in June, but data undoubtedly did not exist the preceding November when the budget was prepared.

The Many-But-Small-Sales Business

This type of business must develop sales budgets from models and trends, because specific data on individual customers are of no value. This is true whether orders are meaningful or not.

The epitome of the many-but-small type of business is probably the fast food restaurant. Operations are quite standardized. How should the owner of a chain of such restaurants budget? The operating costs are quite predictable from models, to which must be added data and trends on local variables: rent, utilities, starting wages, etc.

To predict sales, the owner must consider local demographics, traffic patterns, economy, competition, number and newness of products, and advertising and sales promotion. Again, all these can change quickly, so trends must be questioned. Clearly, the sales of the only fast food restaurant in town can change quickly if two other fast food outlets open nearby.

For this type of business, monthly budgeting is needed, and many owners continually look at numbers. The information must be available to allow quick response to disappointing results, e.g., more advertising, price decreases, special sales promotions, and increased training for improved service.

Thus, the OEFs and assumptions are applicable to this type

of business, too. Sometimes this can be true with a vengeance. A publicized case of food poisoning half a continent away in a same-brand restaurant could significantly decrease sales for a time.

When the owner of the chain of fast food restaurants contemplates opening a new unit, the reasoning involved is similar to that in the budgeting process. The owner probably determines cost first; after checking local conditions, he or she can predict the costs of a new unit accurately. The owner then must decide whether he or she believes the sales will be sufficient to give the desired return. To do this, the owner consciously or unconsciously reviews the same orders and sales drivers that were examined in budgeting.

Indeed, the fast food restaurant chain lends itself so well to modeling, both for budgeting and management, that the concern must be overreliance on numbers. In this business, as with every other, there is no substitute in management for operating knowledge, familiarity, and experience.

Predicting Costs

Predicting costs is the bulk of the number-crunching work of budgeting. Of all bugeting tasks, this is the most company-specific. There are no general algorithms that will tell an engineering manager how much it will cost to design a product, or a manufacturing manager how much it will cost to assemble it. Good cost predictions ultimately depend on the knowledge, intelligence, and experience of the managers involved. However, as in other budgeting activities, there are applicable general principles, in this case two. Properly grounding the cost predictions in these principles will maximize the value of the participants' contributions.

The first general principle is, again: Use data, trends, and models properly. The second is: Base cost predictions on firm understanding of organization activities, outputs, cost drivers, and the relationships between them.

Estimating cost for the budget is easier than predicting orders and sales, but it is not generally problem-free. Some estimating is just poorly done. In addition, poor cost prediction is often motivated, and made worse, by the psychological problems in budgeting that were discussed in Chapter 5. The psychological aspects of the budgeting process make many submitters forecast costs that are higher than they should be. On the other hand, when a submitter is trying to "sell" something to his or her superior, cost estimates may well be too low. The antidote to these problems is to be more deliberate and demanding in the proper use of the two general principles for estimating cost.

Data, Trends, and Models

Some costs are always directly predictable from data. Rent is a simple example. Costs of most things that have been done before are in this category: mature product assembly, restaurant personnel costs, tax return preparation, etc. Things for which costs change slowly, such as office supplies and payroll expense, should be closely predictable from data. Things "bought" in predictable amounts at established prices become data as soon as the price is known: utilities, taxes, audit fees, etc. Where valid data is in hand, it is always what should be used.

Trends are valuable for predicting the costs of factors under management's control, but trends in the pertinent outside environment must be questioned. Factory learning curve trends are an example of the former. The costs of purchased material are an example of the latter; just because costs have increased 5 percent per year for the last three years does not automatically mean that they will do so again next year. Conditions affecting the company's suppliers must be analyzed, and the prices of purchased material are candidates for an assumption if purchased material is important.

Models come into play in predicting costs mostly for new activities, or new ways to do old activities. When automation is to be substituted for labor, a cost model for the automated approach is the usual and proper way to justify the capital expenditure involved. A supermarket chain will model projected costs of a new store on knowledge and data of existing supermarkets and on local conditions for costs such as rent and utilities. This will be done as part of the decision concerning whether to open that new store.

Grounding the cost numbers properly in data, analyzed

trends, and models is also the best way to minimize the psychological component of the budgeting process and the emotional content of budget reviews. In discussing the numbers in budget reviews, note the following:

- *Data* should be shown to support predictions based on that data. Deviations from data need to be explained.
- When *trends* are used, the submitter should both show the applicable trends and explain the reasoning that concludes that the trend will continue.
- Predictions based on *models* should be supported by explaining the model. Conclusions that deviate from the model must be justified.

Activities, Outputs, and Cost Drivers

Rigorous use of the relationships among activities, outputs, and cost drivers is the second requirement for properly grounding cost predictions. The company and every unit in it can be described by their activities, inputs, and outputs, from which cost drivers can be obtained. For the company, the outputs are product shipments and services rendered, expressed financially as sales. The cost drivers include the types and characteristics of products and services; characteristics of customers and suppliers; location of customers, suppliers, and the company; laws and regulations; and procedures and processes. At the other extreme, the output of the mailroom is the number of pieces delivered versus time, while the cost drivers are typically the amount of mail received and sent and locations to be covered.

Predicting costs relates directly back to choosing the best budget format (Chapter 9). Flexible budgeting, activity-based costing, and activity-based assignment of G&A and corporate costs are all essentially ways to get and apply better knowledge of important activity and cost driver relationships. These relationships are the proper basis for cost predictions.

Chapter 2 included the example of the customer sevice manager in the Growth Division of QRS, whose workload was steadily increasing. However, she could not overcome the cost-cutting mentality of her division general manager and the president, and got no cost increase in her budget for the next year. If she had related her costs, using data and analyzed trends, to specific output measures (e.g., number and location of customers, mean time to repair), her plea for increased costs would have been intellectually based, rather than emotional. She would have had a better chance of getting approval for the 10 percent expense increase that was needed. If the increase had still not been approved because of other pressures, her superiors would have clearly understood her plight and lowered their expectations of customer service accordingly.

All managers should give a substantial role in cost budgeting to financial analysis people. Operating people are inclined to miss some elements of cost in a given situation. The budget analyst from accounting is expert in recognizing *all* elements of cost in any endeavor. Indeed, managers should have a general rule that they will accept cost estimates only from accounting, particularly for any new activity. (The important position of budget analyst is further discussed in Chapter 12.)

Finally, costs should be budgeted and controlled on the input side (payroll costs, material costs, etc.) rather than on the accountant's output side (expense, inventory, variances, etc.). This is automatic in flexible budgeting and activity-based costing, as discussed in Chapter 9. However, if the company is still managing on the basis of gross margin and overhead rates, functional managers should deal directly with actual costs and their actual descriptions. Leave the output side of the budget to the accountants, because output parameters do not lead directly to cause and effect. For example, in a manufacturing business, some labor cost goes into or comes out of inventory each month. Knowing the labor that appears on the profit and loss statement as expense does not tell the manager much about the cost of labor that month. More or less may have been spent than is shown, depending on whether inventory went up or down. The manager needs labor *input* to know how much was spent.

Modeling

Modeling is another huge subject about which many books have been written. Extensive treatment of the subject is beyond the scope of this book. The concern here is the application of models to budgeting, not sophisticated modeling itself. The discussion is directed toward application of modeling to budgets for people not very familiar with modeling.

Again, mathematical models are equations or sets of equations describing the relationships among parameters; they predict results for given values of related parameters. It was previously said that the equation

$$\text{Profit} = \text{Sales} - \text{Expense}$$

or

$$P = S - E$$

is a model, although obviously too simple to be of much value in budgeting. However, the expansion of only one term yields a model that, although still very simple, has a specific use. If expense E is expanded into variable expense E_v and fixed expense E_f, the above equation becomes

$$P = S - (E_v + E_f)$$

Since contribution margin m can be expressed as

$$m = (S - E_v)/S$$

then

$$mS = S - E_v$$

and, substituting mS for $S - E_v$, the equation for profit can be written as

$$P = mS - E_f$$

That is, profit equals contribution margin times sales minus fixed expenses. This is directly useful as a gross determinant of the breakeven point of the business. If we set profit to zero, the sales at which the business will break even for given values of contribution margin and fixed expense is

$$S = E_f/m$$

Thus, if margin is 40 percent, the sales figure needed to break even is 2.5 times the fixed expense.

This example illustrates that even simple models can give quick insight into the business, showing variabilities and dependencies. Every model involves some approximation of complex reality, and simple models involve a higher degree of approximation. Therefore, the user of such simple models must understand the underlying reality, so that he or she will understand the applicability and limitations of the model. (It is better to use even simple models for budgeting than to stretch data or trends beyond the point where they are meaningful.)

The foregoing simple breakeven model requires insertion of one value for contribution margin m. In the real world, there are various products and services and different terms and prices, so the single value of m must be an approximation. However, this particular approximation can be remedied easily enough by replacing the single average m with the margins of each type of sale. For the purpose of simplicity in algebra, assume the business in question sells only three products, denoted by subscripts, with each product always sold at the margin m_1, m_2, or m_3. Since margins are ratios, they cannot be simply added to get total margin m_t, but profits can be added:

$$P_t = P_1 + P_2 + P_3$$

or

$$P_t = m_t S_t - E_{f_2} = m_1 S_1 - E_{f1} + m_2 S_2 - E_{f_2} + m_3 S_3 - E_{f_3}$$

Since

$$E_{f_t} = E_{f_1} + E_{f_2} + E_{f_3}$$

and

$$S_t = S_1 + S_2 + S_3$$

then

$$m_t = (m_1 S_1 + m_2 S_2 + m_3 S_3)/S_t$$

This expression for m_t can be substituted into the breakeven equation for m, $S = E_f/m$. The resulting equation allows one to compute breakeven points for different product mixes.

(Relative to the discussion in Chapter 9 of fixed and variable cost budgeting, note that such a simple breakeven analysis could not be done using gross margin rather than contribution margin. In that case, each product carries a proportion of fixed expense with it. Gross margin for each product varies with total sales, because fixed expense is spread by formula—such as direct labor content—over each sale. Thus a breakeven model would be much more complicated.)

With the widespread use of personal computers, there is no reason not to expand such models as far as necessary to achieve the required degree of realism. A business might have twenty or thirty product/price combinations. Even this many can be easily set up in a simple spreadsheet program and "what if" analyses done with different product and price mixes. On the other hand, if the business has thousands of product/price combinations, as many distributors or retailers might have, the modeler would approximate reality by grouping the thousands into a manageable number of *types*. If the types can be chosen so that this simplification is a good approximation, the resulting equation will yield worthwhile results.

Budgeting Models

Models used in budgeting are generally of four types: orders/ sales, profit, cost, and cash flow. An example of an orders/sales model was presented earlier in this chapter in the section "Generating the Numbers." This is the most speculative type of budgeting model, because orders/sales are the most difficult to predict.

The breakeven model just discussed is an example of a profit model. Ordinarily, however, a profit model must include more expense terms and their relationships to be useful in budgeting.

If a machine shop uses activity-based costing to group its expenses, the profit of each product might be:

Profit = Sales − Unit Expense − Batch Expense − Product Expense
− (a portion of) Facility Expense

Then the terms of this equation could be expanded to express the specific cost driver relationships that are found. Batch expense, for example, would be a function of setup time, production runs, and material movements.

Unit expense could be expressed in terms of sales, but product expense is independent of the sales level. Batch expense has a stepwise relationship with product sales. If facility expense is allocated to each product, the portion a particular product bears depends on the basis for allocation used. (Allocating facility expense on the basis of square feet used and utilities consumed is more realistic than a sales-related allocation.) Then total profit would be the summation of profits for all the individual products produced, or perhaps the summation of all contracts if that is more useful. Most machine shops have many products or contracts, so a realistic model would have many terms. Again, personal computers make it much easier to deal with the complexity that comes from many terms in the model.

Cost models are basically functional activity models. Modeling activities, inputs, and outputs allows costs for different levels of outputs to be readily obtained. For many service functions—bank teller operations, waiting on restaurant customers, for example—the activities are transactions plus support for those transactions—food, table setting, and the like for restaurants; account information, approvals, and the availability of currency and forms for bank tellers. The required outputs are usually the important cost drivers for such services: the number of customers and their distribution over time (peaking factor). Modeling the main and supporting transactions in the time dimension, and relating time to the cost of the people involved, yields the cost of serving a given distribution of customers with a given level of service. If there is an average transaction time of fifteen minutes, ten servers are needed to ensure that a peak of twenty simultaneous customers will be served, each with no more than a fifteen-minute wait. Real situations have more complexity, such as widely varying transaction times. The point is that the activity can be described by equations and put on a personal computer, and the cost of different levels of service for different numbers and distribution of customers can be determined easily. Each function will have its own, unique cost model, of course, and the key, again, is activities, inputs, and outputs.

Models are particularly useful in predicting cash flow. The many-but-small-sales business must use models because specific data are unavailable or not useful. Even in the few-but-large-sales business, however, the uncertainties in orders and sales data grow rapidly when converted into cash flow. In such a business, if there is a plus or minus three-month uncertainty in the timing of the order and shipment, there may be another one- to three-month uncertainty concerning when the customer will pay, particularly if installation and testing is required for customer acceptance. Thus, a three-month order time uncertainty becomes, by taking the extremes of the uncertainties of both order time and payment time, a possible eight-month window for receiving payment.

It must be understood, however, that in the few-but-large-sales business, the model will depict only the average situation. Real cash flow can deviate widely from that average when receipts are few and large. Thus, models are used not because they are specific predictors but because they give more accurate forecasts than relying on data beyond the time those data are meaningful. The actual extremes of cash flow are difficult to predict for the few-but-large-sales business. The best approach is to use specific data for as long as they are applicable and rely on a model for the longer-term future. Then, understanding that this model depicts only the average, ensure that cash will be available for reasonable extremes of slow-paying customers.

The simplest cash flow model is:

Cash Flow = Profit − Non-cash Profit + Non-cash Expense − Capital
Expenditures − Change in Working Capital

Non-cash profit and expense terms are needed to remove from profit any items that do not involve cash at the time. Unless there are unusual circumstances, that largest non-cash item is depreciation and amortization. The required working capital (generally accounts receivable, inventory, and accounts payable) usually varies with the level of sales, so the change in working capital in a given year varies with the change in sales. If we make the simplifying assumption that change in working capital equals a constant times the change in sales, or

$$\Delta W = k \, \Delta S$$

we can use this simple cash model to find the point at which a new, growing business or product line will reach positive cash flow. Intuitively, if sales grow rapidly, it will take considerable sales and profit to overcome the rapidly growing need for working capital, and this simple model shows the relationship. With cash flow F, depreciation and amortization D, capital expenditures C, and using the previously determined profit expression $P = mS - E_f$, as well as the above expression for change in working capital ΔW, the cash flow model becomes:

$$F = mS - E_f + D - C - k \, \Delta S$$

Setting $F = 0$ and solving for S shows the relationship between sales level (S) and sales growth (ΔS) for the point at which cash flow passes through zero going in the positive direction as sales grow:

$$S = (k \, \Delta S + E_f + C - D) / m$$

That is, a new business with rapid sales growth, high fixed expense and capital expenditures, and low margin will have to attain a high level of sales before the business stops needing cash and starts generating it.

As in profit models, to be useful in budgeting, cash flow models are normally more complex than this. It may be more useful to model cash flow as a table of receipts and expenditures rather than as equations. For example, for a product being built and sold, construct columns that represent months. Enter purchased material received in the amounts and months expected.

Offsetting those numbers by an amount representing the time before invoices are paid yields expenditures for purchased material. Enter labor dollars and other expenses charged to the product as they are paid. Enter expected shipments of the products by month. Offsetting these shipments by the receivables time yields expected receipts from the product. Subtracting material, labor, and other expenditures from these receipts gives monthly cash flow. As an example, consider cash flow for an $800,000, one-year contract for a manufactured product:

(Numbers in thousands of dollars)												
Months	J	F	M	A	M	J	J	A	S	O	N	D
Material received	30	30	30	30	30	30	30	30				
Material paid*		30	30	30	30	30	30	30	30			
Labor/other expense			20	20	20	20	20	20	20	20		
Shipments				100	100	100	100	100	100	100	100	
Receipts**					100	100	100	100	100	100	100	100
Cash flow***	0	(30)	(50)	(50)	50	50	50	50	50	80	100	100
Cumulative cash flow	0	(30)	(80)	(130)	(80)	(30)	20	70	120	200	300	400

*One month after material received
**Two months after shipments
***Cash flow = Receipts − Material paid − Labor/other expense

Modeling many or all aspects of a business is recommended, both for budgeting and for the insight that models give to fundamental relationships and dependencies in the business. Any functional manager will benefit from modeling the function's activities, inputs, and outputs.

To get the best numerical content in a budget, first generate the entire budget from models. Then, for the near time period in which data are meaningful, override the model with that data. Finally, further check and possibly modify the model with questioned trends and expected changes in the OEFs (if the latter were not included in the model).

Modeling the Company and/or Division(s)

A company or division business model relating the important factors that affect return on investment (ROI) is useful for budgeting and other planning activities. It is specifically recommended here as an insightful labor-saving device to generate a preliminary budget. However, once in hand, its value to the organization will be much greater: It will clearly show members of an organization important relationships that were not obvious before.

For example, most manufacturing professionals have excellent knowledge of how to make things, fair to good knowledge of what affects profitability, but poor knowledge of all the elements of ROI. ROI, of course, is the ultimate criterion in deciding among alternative courses of action: Which one will give the best return on the money invested? A typical production manager would like to order inventory so that all the required material is on hand before a production run begins. This minimizes production problems and probably minimizes production cost. However, it means that excess inventory will be carried for a period of time, increasing the investment in the project. If everything else is equal, this will reduce ROI and make the project less desirable. But, this cannot be said categorically without knowing the potential cost increases resulting from production line shutdowns if just-in-time inventory is attempted and does not work. To intelligently balance the effects of excess inventory versus potential production line problems, one needs to analyze the operation, which requires a model.

The business model culminates in an equation for ROI, which can take different forms but can be expressed simply as profit divided by funds employed, ordinarily capital plus working capital. To build the model, one must summarize the different activities into major types, selected so that each different kind of financial activity is represented. A car dealership, for example, might choose new car sales, used car sales, service, and leasing; each of these has quite different financial and business characteristics. Then the relationship to profit and investment must be established for each type of activity. These are all then worked into a series of equations leading to ROI.

In general, for each category,

$$\text{Profit} = \text{Sales} - \text{Expense}$$
$$\text{Working Capital} = \text{Receivables} + \text{Inventory} + \text{Payables}$$
$$\text{Receivables} = \text{Receivable Day} \times \text{Sales}$$
$$\text{Inventory} = \text{Inventory Days} \times \text{Cost of Sales}$$
$$\text{Payables} = \text{Payable Days} \times \text{Purchased Material}$$
$$\text{ROI} = \text{Profit}/(\text{Capital} + \text{Working Capital})$$

Capital is the sum of the depreciated value of equipment, tools, facilities (if they are owned), etc., employed for the category in question. The various "days" are constants from experience or policy that describe how long after a sale payment is received, how long inventory is held (actually, how much is on hand relative to sales), and how long after its receipt material payment is made. "Receivable days," for example, is the average number of days after a sale for payment to be received; it is usually computed as 365 times accounts receivable, divided by sales. The right sides of the ROI equation for each category are summed to obtain the ROI of the total business, after including the remainder of company expense and capital that is not assignable to any of the product categories.

The key to successful use of such a business model is in understanding that it is an approximation, never precisely accurate, but that it will yield useful information and insight. The chief insight will be the time value of money, which is never obtained from the usual operating calculations. The car dealer has working capital invested in a used car from the time he or she pays for it until payment is received after the sale. (The receivable, inventory, and payable days are a way of expressing this total "investment time," which relates to the profit parameters of sales and expense.) Depending on the magnitude of the profit and capital, this working capital may have a strong influence on ROI. Minimizing the collection time and inventory and maximizing payment time is important in improving ROI in most businesses.

Use of a business ROI model is the correct way to determine how much of a sales discount to give for early receipt of payment, and also how much of a purchase discount should be taken. Consider a sales discount. In the ROI equation, the lower sales (because of the discount) decrease profit in the numerator. However, the shorter collection or receivable time also decreases working capital in the denominator. Substituting the proper numbers for all elements into the ROI equation, one can solve for the new combination of (lower) profit and (lower) working capital, which yields the same ROI as for the values before the discount. From the answer for lower profit, one can calculate the percentage of discount for a given (shorter) collection time, which will yield the same ROI as before. Clearly, any discount less than this percentage will result in a higher ROI than before discount. Any such discount is thus desirable if it can yield the stipulated shorter collection time.

The reasoning in determining a purchase discount is exactly the opposite: The calculation will yield the minimum discount that can be taken without lowering ROI. The correct answer depends on using the correct numbers for the particular business, of course. This analysis often concludes that higher sales discounts for early receipt of payment should be given than seems right intuitively or is generally believed. Similarly, purchase discounts often should be *higher* than those generally offered to make sense for the buyer. ROI is the correct parameter on which to base these conclusions, because it is a measure of how much business can be done and how much profit made on a given investment, which is the ultimate business question.

FUNCTIONAL MANAGERS: SURMOUNTING A POOR BUDGETING PROCESS

There is little more to be said about budget content. The budget finally comes down to numbers, and they must be "the best that they can be." All aspects of making the proper use of data, trends, models, and input and output relationships are directly applicable to every functional manager.

The most common content problem in a poor budgeting process may be a distrust of models and a corresponding demand for data to support a budget. A sales manager might be required to support a fourth-quarter orders budget with specific customer names, even though he or she knows the natural predictive cycle (the time for which data are meaningful) is only six months. A director may demand a cash flow forecast for the next year's fourth quarter that includes specific receipts and disbursements, even though this borders on fantasy for the particular company.

Another kind of problem may result from a management practice that, on its face, appears to be good. I once had a superior whose budget reviews were only concerned with trends. He required plots of various budget elements (particular types of costs, sales, orders, etc.) over a number of years, plus the next year's proposed budget number. Only those elements for which the next year's number violated the trend needed to be discussed. This sounds like a good way to avoid wasting time by concentrating on the things that are changing. Actually, however, all trends need to be questioned all the time. Fortunes in every walk of life have been lost by not recognizing the sudden change or invalidation of a trend. There were, at times, problems in numbers that did not deviate from the trend, and some of those that did change were a waste of time to discuss. (How much better it is if a superior's basis of review concentration is a thorough discussion of OEFs and assumptions!)

The functional manager obviously must be responsive to his or her superiors' desires. If they want data or trends, he or she must be ready with them. The recommendation for the functional manager in such a situation is threefold. First, however he or she must present them, the budgeted numbers must be properly developed from data, trends, and models. Second, the functional manager should attempt to steer the reviews and the process toward the proper use of these three sources of budget numbers. Third, he or she should be forthright concerning what is being done and why.

11

Encouraging Excellence: The Beauty of Gap Analysis

The management of every company owes its owners its best efforts to achieve the second composite objective of a powerful budgeting process (discussed in Chapter 4), a budget that plans "the best results achievable . . . consistent with acceptable risk and the long-term health of the business. . . ." This is not easy to do, nor is it trivial. As discussed previously, all the obstacles to good budgeting are arrayed against this objective. The conflict in objectives, the uncertainty of the future, the uncontrollability of outside factors, measurement techniques, and the psychology inherent in budgeting all push budgeting participants to plan lower performance than is achievable.

The "best results achievable" will never happen automatically. They must be planned for and managed. Encouragement of excellence in everything the company does thus becomes one of the primary budgeting requirements. Therefore, the budgeting process needs a deliberate technique, at every level and at every step, that will promote excellent performance and push the participants to strive for the best results realistically possible. The recommended technique is gap analysis, a general tool for strategic planning, performance improvement, and problem solving.

Gap Analysis Defined

Gap analysis begins with identification of a parameter of concern or interest. This parameter, called the gap dimension, can be anything from orders, sales, or profit to quality defects, proficiency in a particular skill, or factory rework levels. Two future projections of this parameter are then made: (1) the desired goal value and (2) the expected result of retaining the status quo, i.e., of continuing to do the same things in the same way. These two projections define a *gap*, the difference between the goal and the expected status quo result. It is often useful to visualize and communicate this gap in graph form. The all-important final step in gap analysis is to develop action programs to fill the gap, i.e., to reach the desired goal.

To illustrate the concept, assume that a division general manager is committed to a goal of increasing profit 15 percent per year. The best information from data and questioned trends, modified by assumptions about the outside environmental factors, convinces him or her that if the division keeps doing what it is doing, profit will hardly grow at all. The general manager has identified a gap between the goal of 15 percent profit growth and the expected status quo result of zero growth. This gap will not close by itself, but only by action on the part of the organization. Defining this gap gives the general manager the means to state and communicate the problem, begin considering alternatives, and develop action programs to reach the goal.

To look at another application of gap analysis, assume that an accounting organization takes ten working days to close the books each month. For a number of reasons, hardly anyone is happy with that length of time, and the controller and key accounting people address the problem. In this case, the goal is not obvious and requires some analysis and trade-offs. Ideally, everyone would want a one-day closing, but the goal must be possible, preferably challenging but achievable. Assume that six days is chosen as an acceptable and practical goal. The gap dimension is closing time, the goal is six days, and the expected status quo result, if nothing is done differently, will continue to be ten days. The problem is thus defined. Alternatives such as new procedures, earlier cutoffs, and increased automation can be investigated. The goal and the gap focus the investigation, facilitate communication, help select the best alternatives, and drive the development and implementation of action programs to solve the problem.

Not all gaps can be filled. Original goals sometimes prove to be unrealistic and must be lowered. Thus, an iterative process may be required for goals and actions until a realistic combination is developed. The original goal should be retained; that the organization believes that it cannot be met, although it is desirable, is important information for top management, telling them the limits of probable accomplishment. If the goal is important, top-management action is required to introduce conditions that will allow goal fulfillment. Either that must be done or objectives and strategies must be changed.

Gap analysis is applicable at every level of the organization and to almost all business parameters. The beauty of gap analysis lies in the many ways it can be applied, while giving all participants a common language in which to deal objectively with goals, problems, and actions. A set of specific, quantified gaps and related action programs throughout a company will generate enthusiasm and focus the entire organization on the pursuit of excellence. It sends a message of willingness to do the new and exciting things necessary to ensure the health of the company in its ever-changing environment.*

Gap Analysis Applied to Budgeting

The application of gap analysis to budgeting is similar to any other application, except that the time horizon is specifically the next (budget) year.

The process is begun by selecting the parameters or dimensions for which the gaps are to be constructed. At the top levels of a company, the dimensions are commonly the most important financial parameters, such as profit. At lower levels, the dimension is often the most important output of the particular function: orders by the sales department, product performance by engineering, number of new hires by recruiting, etc. Many gap dimensions should result from particular problems the company

---

*I am indebted to Michael Kami, an outstanding strategic management consultant, for introducing me to gap analysis some years ago. Further information on the subject is available in his book, *Trigger Points* (New York: McGraw-Hill, 1988).

wants resolved. In Chapter 9, an example of a purchasing cost driver was simply the number of purchase orders. If purchasing costs are a particular concern, a gap analysis whose dimension is volume of purchase orders would be valuable.

The universe of potentially useful gap dimensions is huge. There are only two requirements for their selection. The first is that the dimension must be something that the pertinent management can control, influence, and change directly by its actions. It would be useless for a functional organization to do a gap analysis of profit, because profit is influenced by so many things about which a function can do nothing. Second, any given organization should do only a small number of gap analyses. The purpose of the analysis is to define, direct, and focus action. If many gaps are constructed, the result will be to defocus the organization as it tries to go in too many directions toward too many goals at once. Gap analysis should be reserved for the really important results and problems; often one gap for a function is enough for any budget year.

The second step is to select the goal for the budget year for the chosen gap dimension. This may be obvious and concurrent with selection of the gap dimension, or it may require considerable analysis. If a company has a continuing objective of 15 percent profit growth per year, both the profit gap dimension and the next year's goal are stated in the same breath on the first day of the process. On the other hand, in the purchasing costs example of a gap analysis for "number of purchase orders," much analysis was required to establish that as a most useful gap dimension, and considerably more analysis is required to set a proper goal for the year.

As illustrated later, there is often information value in initially challenging an organization with an unrealistic goal. However, the final goal setting used in the budgeting process must be realistic. If the gap dimensions are irrelevant, or if the goals are too low or too high, the requirement of encouraging excellence will not be met. Final goals must be specific; they must represent something that the particular manager can change through his or her actions; and they must be at the ambitious end of realism. Also, all goals must support and be consistent with company strategies and plans.

Fortunately, the gap analysis process itself sets up motivation that encourages ambitious goals. Managers like to be asked to state the job they would really like to accomplish, or the capability that they would really like their organizations to have. Any manager likes an opportunity to tell what he or she could accomplish and to "sell" a program to get there. Also, most managers will step up to ambitious goals if they believe that their problems are understood and that, therefore, their performance measurement will be realistic. Thus, the inherent budgeting problems of conflicting objectives, measurement, and psychological factors may appear in the goal-setting process; however, they can be dealt with because of the specificity of the subject matter and the positive motivation that the gap analysis process fosters. The remainder of the task of setting good goals, as usual, rests with the understanding, competence, and judgment of the submitting and reviewing managers.

The initial gap analysis activities— selecting gap dimensions and goals—can be validly approached from different directions. One way is for budgeting participants at every level to think through their objectives and problems to define proper gap dimensions and goals for their organizations. Another useful way to begin is from the top down. The president may ask the divisions, for example, "What must you do, and what must happen in the outside world, to increase profit by 20 percent next year?" Whether possible or not, this can lead to useful, mind-stretching analysis. If both the reasoning from OEFs to assumptions and management actions are properly studied, the results are a wealth of useful information for the president. Such results can help the president place "bets" on the future in an informed fashion. An iterative combination of top-down and bottom-up approaches is a third way to approach the process and may be the best in many situations. Here the objective is to hammer out the most useful gap dimensions and realistic goals by iteration between superiors and subordinates.

After selecting the dimensions and goals for gap analysis, the third step in the process is to define the expected status quo result for the budget year. Status quo means taking no new action to change results in the gap dimension; in other words, what is expected to happen if current actions are continued? A common source of the status quo prediction for functional gap analysis is the recent trend modified by expected events and actions that are outside the gap dimension but will influence it; in other words, "questioned" trends are used. In the purchasing example of "number of purchase orders," one might expect the status quo number to remain constant. Or, if the business is changing or growing, the number may grow unless new action is taken. On the other hand, a profit gap analysis for the company requires that the full range of work of the assumptions process (Chapter 8) be done before the status quo expectation can be stated.

The penultimate step of gap analysis is to determine action programs to close the gap and the predicted effects of each. Good action programs are the direct result of the gap analysis—and the reason for it. Proper action programs are facilitated by the specificity and focus that gap analysis provides. They are directed at specific, measurable results and are done by the people with the best knowledge and ability to attain those results.

The fifth and final step, developing and inserting the actual numbers into the budget, is mechanical and almost effortless if good gap analyses have been done. If the company is doing good budgeting, the gap analysis goals will be supported by action programs that make their attainment probable. The gap analysis goals (not status quo) and the action resources required are the numbers that should be put in the budget.

An important benefit of gap analysis is that it provides a common language for communication through the entire management hierarchy. If planned actions and problems are communicated by means of specific gap dimensions, goals, status quo expectations, and resulting gaps, everyone can quickly get on the same page and misunderstandings will be minimized. Business needs and practices are usually sophisticated and their benefits abstract. The importance of a functional goal to the overall company results is often not obvious; similarly, the right functional goal to support overall company goals is also often not obvious. The language of gap analysis will help focus everyone on all the right things.

The following examples illustrate the variety of possible applications for gap analysis in budgeting and the requirements and benefits of some of the different kinds of analysis.

Example: The Value of Negative Information

In Chapter 2, the budgeting problems of the Growth Division of the fictitious QRS Company were presented. The division general manager of Growth faced the problem that his division's profit had fallen short of a five-year projection presented two years ago. He felt strong pressure to get back on the projected growth path. However, unforeseen economic problems in Growth's market and increased material costs, plus the perception that he had to increase indirect expense to protect continuing sales, convinced him that the next year's results would be disappointing. The Growth general manager also believed that he had a promising new product that could get the division back on the desired growth path in a few years, but proper pursuit of that product would severely lower next year's profit.

His solution was to increase orders beyond what he believed likely and to add only part of the indirect expense and new product development expense he felt he needed. As a result, he bluffed through his budget and failed in his responsibility to communicate an important problem to the president and the board of directors. They unknowingly approved a budget that had little likelihood of being met.

How much better it would have been for the QRS Company if he had performed and presented a gap analysis of his problem! Using profit as the parameter, the goal would have been simply the next year's profit from the two-year-old projection. He could have shown this graphically, together with the previous year's profit and the current year's expected profit. He would then have been able to build his status quo projection of next year's profit by extrapolating from (1) profits for last year and this year, (2) the economic problems in Growth's market, (3) the increased material costs, and (4) the need to increase indirect expense to protect continuing sales. The result would have been a sizable gap that the general manager should have stated he could not fill.

Then he could have shifted into a strategic gap analysis showing the remaining three years of the five-year projection. This would have given him the proper platform to advocate increased development spending for the promising new product, even though next year's profit would be lowered. His strategic action plan, then, would have been to increase development and indirect expense to weather the current economic problems in his market, with the promise of good growth again in three years.

This entire process would have presented the real problem in terms readily understood by the president and the board of directors. The Growth manager might not have got what he wanted; the president and the board might have decided not to bet on Growth's future again. They might have told him to cut expenses where he could and maximize next year's profit. But it would have been an informed decision, with the best facts and judgments presented. Thus, the decision made would probably have been the best one possible for QRS. The presentation and decision process would have been much better than the one shown in Chapter 2.

Example: **Choosing the Right Gap Dimension**

The gap dimensions or parameters analyzed must be ones the manager can act upon, influence, or control. Consider an investor relations function in a public company. The company in question has concluded that it will need to raise money within the next two years and that some of it should be raised by selling equity. To do this, the company would like very much to have a higher price for its common stock. The president and the board feel that the stock is undervalued, and investor relations is told to plan and budget a program for next year that will have a good effect on the stock price. (Unfortunately, many presidents and boards believe that their stock is always undervalued, whether it really is or not. For purposes of this example, the assumption will be that this time they are right.)

What is the proper gap dimension for investor relations? Should it be the stock price? Emphatically not! Prices of common stock are influenced by many forces, none of which are totally understood at any particular time. The company's stock price may go up or down, independent of anything that investor relations does. Further, investor relations cannot turn bad news into good news. Therefore, to attempt to define a status quo stock price and a goal stock price for one year hence would be a meaningless exercise. Such a gap would give no information for planning investor relations actions.

However, it is generally accepted that "sponsorship" by important securities analysts helps maximize a stock price for given conditions, i.e., the more the respected analysts who comment favorably on a stock, the more it will be bought. Therein lies a proper dimension for investor relations gap analysis: the number of important securities analysts who follow the company's stock. The status quo number one year hence may be the same as the current number. A reasonable goal may be to double that number. The definition needs to be completed by stating what constitutes an "important" securities analyst (perhaps from a list of major research and brokerage firms) and what "follow the stock" means (for example, mention in the analyst's written materials).

The first value of this gap analysis comes from the agreement between the president and the investor relations manager that this is the appropriate gap dimension for the needs of the president and the board of directors. It represents a deliberate decision that increasing the number of securities analysts is an appropriate investor relations focus for the next year.

The discussion involved will also reduce anyone's temptation to blame investor relations if the stock price goes down next year. There is a serious point behind this flippant statement: It is important to clarify what superiors and subordinates believe an organization can change versus what it cannot.

Further, identifying the appropriate gap dimension provides a direct basis for an action program for investor relations. This might include more frequent contact and meetings with securities analysts, presentations by the president and the chief financial officer, additional news releases, background papers, and the like. The investor relations budget will follow directly from the action program. The budget will thus be tied to a program directed toward a specific goal, and both performance vis-à-vis this goal and performance vis-à-vis the budget will be easily measurable.

This does not imply that the investor relations manager will be measured only on progress toward this gap analysis goal. Management is not that simple, and quality and quantity of output, the handling of crises, general investor relations, and so on will all be part of the manager's appraisal. However, the beauty of gap analysis is the focus it provides and communicates to all concerned about an important goal and direction for next year. Multiple gap dimensions are also possible. If this company were also particularly concerned about poor stockholder relations, another gap analysis could be constructed to attack this problem and would communicate a second focus for next year's efforts.

Another value of the gap analysis in this example is the major benefit in intramanagement communications. How to get a higher stock price is a fuzzy, controversial subject that will interest every director as well as top management. The whole process, from defining the gap dimension through developing the action program and budget, will marvelously focus and direct what could have been chaotic discussions. Gap analysis, again, puts everyone on the same page and reduces fuzzy problems to specific dimensions that can be discussed and attacked.

Example: Gap Analysis as a Problem-Solving Tool

In this example, a management information systems (MIS) manager, as she begins her budgeting effort, has a major concern: Requests for modifications in manufacturing software have increased so rapidly that her programmers can hardly do anything else. The vice-president of manufacturing is also unhappy, because he cannot get done the things he wants done, and the excuse is usually that his people are waiting for the programmers to finish the needed software modifications. The cursory conclusion would be that the MIS manager needs to budget and hire more programmers to keep up with the increasing load. This will be expensive and will not make anyone happy.

Manufacturing was a full partner in selecting the manufacturing software two years earlier. The MIS manager knows that this software is good and that similar factories use it with little or no modification. Therefore, either her "customers" in manufacturing use many customized procedures, or they do not know the software well enough to use it to get what they need.

The MIS manager and her key people study the problem and conclude that its main source is a deterioration in the knowledge of the software among manufacturing personnel. As people in user positions have turned over or been promoted, the new ones have not been as well trained. They ask for programming modifications to solve their perceived problems, so the programmers get too busy to do training, and the problem gets worse. The MIS manager takes her diagnosis to the vice-president of manufacturing and gets the latter's key people involved. They soon concur that the software is not being used well and that more and more modifications are not a good solution.

With this insight into the problem, the objective of both organizations becomes maximizing the use of the existing software. The MIS manager structures a gap analysis whose dimension is the number of software modification requests by manufacturing per month. For the status quo result, she plots, monthly, an acceleration of the recent trend. She gets manufacturing to agree to a goal for reducing modification requests, which is expressed as a linear reduction from the status quo graph starting in the second quarter of the following year. Part of the gap definition is that manufacturing's information requirements must be as well and as quickly satisfied as they are currently; in other words, manufacturing agrees to the status quo on its side of the problem for another year.

As in the previous examples, this gap analysis leads directly to pertinent action programs. It provides the planning and communication focus for both manufacturing and MIS and leads to training and education plans and a publicized help desk supplied by MIS to manufacturing users. Manufacturing sets up a procedure whereby its own experts and MIS will preapprove future modification requests. The MIS manager, with manufacturing's support, gets approval to engage temporary programmers to help handle the current workload so that her regular programmers can begin the training, education, and help-desk work.

This example again illustrates the value of gap analysis in selecting functional goals, defining useful action programs, and serving as a management communication mechanism. Most of all, it illustrates the value of gap analysis as a multifunctional problem-solving tool. Gap analysis provided the common language and focus that let MIS and manufacturing together define and attack a problem that had plagued them both.

Conclusion: Benefits of Gap Analysis

The budgeting requirement discussed in this chapter—encouraging excellence in everything the company does—is a primary requirement because management owes the company owners its best efforts to plan and achieve the best possible results.

Every company has an obligation to encourage excellence in all its activities. The use of gap analysis is not the only way to do this. However, gap analysis is an unparalleled technique to improve performance and to encourage the best performance possible. The beauty of gap analysis is that it can be applied in so many ways, with so many valuable results, including the following:

- It *does* encourage the best performance possible, by defining proper parameters, fostering ambitious goals for performance in those parameters, and promoting specific actions to meet the goals.
- It has broad application. It can be used in strategic planning, budgeting, and problem solving. A particular gap analysis can be started by top management, by individual contributors, or by anyone in between.
- It provides a direct basis for action programs to satisfy goals and solve problems.
- It supplies a common language for communicating at all levels of management the needs and problems of the business.
- It promotes agreement on important business parameters and goals.
- It clarifies what can be changed by management action and what cannot. As such, it is an answer to the old prayer, "Lord, give me the courage to change what I can, the patience to accept what I cannot change, and the wisdom to know the difference."
- It improves measurement of managers through the aforementioned clarification of things that managers can and cannot change.
- It yields valuable negative information, e.g., that a particular goal is unreasonable, or that its satisfaction is improba-

ble. This fosters management focus on goals and activities which have a better chance for success.

- It is a potent problem-solving tool.

In short, gap analysis provides a well-communicated focus on the parameters and activities that management wishes to emphasize, i.e., those that are most important to the success of the business.

FUNCTIONAL MANAGERS: SURMOUNTING A POOR BUDGETING PROCESS

Gap analysis can be used by any functional manager to improve budgeting, solve problems, and encourage excellence. He or she can use it to explain how a stated goal is unreachable without luck or different ways of doing things.

In a poor budgeting process, the functional manager may wish to use the status quo result, rather than the goal, as the starting budget number. This depends on the particular psychological situation. If the goal is self-imposed, the manager may wish to keep it in reserve for possible budget negotiations with superiors. If the goal was imposed by superiors, that figure should probably be the budget number. In that case, he or she should carefully explain what must be done, and what must happen, for the goal to be met.

The first place for a functional manager to use gap analysis is within his or her own organization. Ordinarily, he or she should explain to the superior what is being done and commit to the gap analysis goals. A more far-reaching application of gap analysis for a functional manager, if the environment allows it, is to propose and promote it for interfunction problems or performance improvement. Most companies have difficulty solving multifunction problems. Gap analysis, particularly as part of budgeting, is a good way to work out these problems.

It is hard to imagine gap analysis being controversial. Disagreements could arise over predicting what the result will be if the status quo is maintained, or the goal might be considered not ambitious enough. However, this is the normal give-and-take of budget negotiations; both sides should welcome the clarity and focus on the issues that gap analysis provides.

Each company function should do at least one gap analysis as part of budgeting. However, none should do very many, or else the result will be loss of focus and "milling around," instead of clarity and improvement.

12

Putting It Together: Process Flow and the Details

The last budgeting requirement is that everything be tied together in a process that flows coherently and fits in all the details effectively and efficiently. The process must be designed so that it addresses all the budgeting requirements and all the objectives and obstacles. It must provide the means to focus on the right things at the right time. It must yield dependable accuracy and consistency with minimal effort. It must deal appropriately with future uncertainty and uncontrollable factors and provide the basis for getting beyond these so that major attention can be paid to the things that management *can* control and influence. Finally, the process must facilitate good communication within the organization.

In Chapters 7 through 11, techniques are presented for satisfying the first five budgeting requirements developed in Chapter 6. These techniques include the strategy/budget continuum; the assumptions process; flexible budgeting, activity-based costing, and the like; use of data, trends, and models and input and output relationships; and gap analysis. This chapter treats satisfaction of the sixth requirement, presenting the budgeting process flow (shown in Figures 1 through 3) for a powerful budgeting process. Then a section discusses the important details. Finally, a discussion of transition provides guidance on appropriate ways to move from an inferior to a powerful budgeting process.

Common Process Flow Problems

The biggest problems with most budgeting processes are that they take too long and generate budget figures too early. A tremendous amount of work goes into budgeting, and budgets often get reviewed and redone more than once. Budgeting is important, but one sometimes gets the impression that managers have no time for decisions related to making, selling, and servicing because they spend all their time in budget meetings. Also, the earlier the numbers are generated, the more the value of the budget deteriorates, simply because the predictions are made for a longer period of time.

The budgeting process recommended here is not necessarily shorter than such problem processes. However, the significant difference is that the preliminary phase of the process is totally devoted to conceptual planning, definition of issues, and identification of parameters and problems on which to focus attention. Only near the end are budget numbers generated. Again, "thinking it through before crunching the numbers" will generate reliable numbers relatively easily.

A particular process-flow problem is the "precision without accuracy" problem. It occurs in multiple forms. One form is starting with raw guesses and presenting the result in six or seven significant figures. Another form is getting very specific about things such as the amount and timing of orders, which can only be guesses. In my experience, this phenomenon is suprisingly widespread. I have never understood why someone would say that "telephone expense next year will be $336,427," when he or she cannot predict it within $40,000 either way. This is a problem in two ways: It misleads the reader or listener into believing that the information is more accurate than it is, and it causes additional work and potential for error because there are more numbers to manipulate. This must be addressed by emphasizing the proper use of data, questioned trends, and models, and by specifying procedures and software properly. For example, computer spreadsheet programs should be instructed to round their computations to the appropriate number of significant figures.

Budgeting Process Inputs

The inputs to the budgeting process are shown on the left side of Figure 1; the first three apply all through the process. *Administrative directions* are the needed guidance on the details and mechanics of putting the budget together. These are described later in "The Details."

The *models* input includes those for return on investment, orders, cash flow, expense, and so forth. Different models are inputs to different parts of the process but are shown in Figure 1 as general inputs for simplicity. The *budget format* input means that the budget must be initially put into the format most useful to management, as discussed in Chapter 9. (This new format must then be carefully communicated together with the reasons for the change; do not assume that it will be automatically understood.) Once the useful format is established, annual reviews need only be cursory.

Figure 1.   Budget process overview.

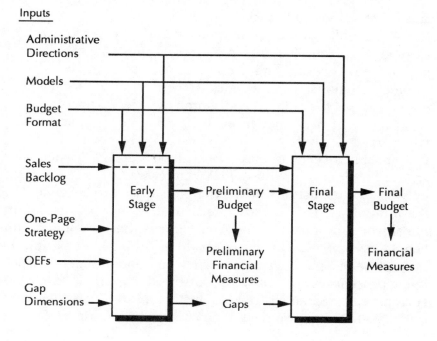

Sales backlog, orders received but not yet filled, is a straight-forward data input to the process of forecasting the next year's sales.

Two strategic inputs, the *one-page strategy* and *outside environmental factors* (OEFs) (along with strategy-based *gap dimensions*), directly integrate strategic planning and the budgeting process. The inputs shown in Figure 1 are the minimum strategic needs of the budgeting process; a major strategic planning process would generate more inputs to budgeting, but the items shown are needed even if no strategic planning has been done. The one-page strategy statement should present the business areas and product lines on which the company will concentrate and their relative priorities, and it should also state the areas or products with which the company will *not* be concerned.

Similarly, the logical place to identify the pertinent outside environmental factors is in strategic planning; but if that has not been done, it must be done as a prelude to budgeting. As noted previously, assumptions proceed from OEFs. Assumptions may be appropriately identified as part of strategic planning, rather than budgeting, but they *must* be developed as part of budgeting if not done before. (Again, identifying important OEFs is a major task only when done for the first time. These will not change much year to year, so only a short review should be required after the first year. The same is not true for assumptions; they must be developed with care each year.)

On the other hand, a good strategic planning process can almost replace the early stage of budgeting. Chapter 7 suggests developing various scenarios based on different sets of assumptions. If this has been done, the early stage of budgeting requires little more than selecting the next-year forecast of one particular scenario. (There should still be a check of sales backlog and orders prospects, and more gap analysis definition should be done.) In fact, this development of different sets of assumptions and scenarios in strategic planning is the ideal way to couple that planning with budgeting. Again, however, the budgeting process presented here shows the minimum inputs from strategic planning, or what is needed strategically for budgeting even if no strategic planning has been done.

The final input to the overall budgeting process is *gap dimen-*

sions, the parameters that will be the subject of gap analysis (e.g., profit, delivery time, quality defects). Desired gap dimensions come from many sources: improvement needs identified in strategic planning or in early-stage budgeting, need for increased capacity in particular functions, general encouragement of excellence, and so on. As such, identification of gap dimensions is an ongoing process, occurring throughout the year. (Figure 2 portrays new gap dimensions identified as a result of various early-stage budgeting activities. For example, an increased sales forecast for a particular product may indicate the need for increased factory throughput of that product, and that throughput would thus become a gap dimension.)

Given that the identification of gap dimensions is essentially a continuous process, there are, however, two times in particular when the organization should pause and take stock. The first is at the beginning of the budgeting process; identified gap dimensions should be reviewed and prioritized at that time, with some discarded and perhaps some added, so that the resulting workload is reasonable. Second, at the end of the early stage, there should be a cutoff on identifying gap dimensions until the following year, together with a similar review of workload and prioritization. This cutoff is required so that the participants can concentrate during the final stage on action programs for the identified gaps. If identification of new gap dimensions continues, no one will have time to develop the action programs to fill the gaps; the action programs, after all, are the reason that gap analysis is done.

Process Overview

A budgeting process for a business for which orders are meaningful (i.e., one in which a customer "orders" goods or services for later delivery, in contrast with most retail stores) is shown in Figure 1. Such a business has activities related to orders that the orders-not-meaningful business does not. The latter type of business would replace orders-related activities with data, questioned trends, and (particularly) modeling that lead to sales budgets.

The process presented is for a company in a single business.

Figure 2. Early-stage process.

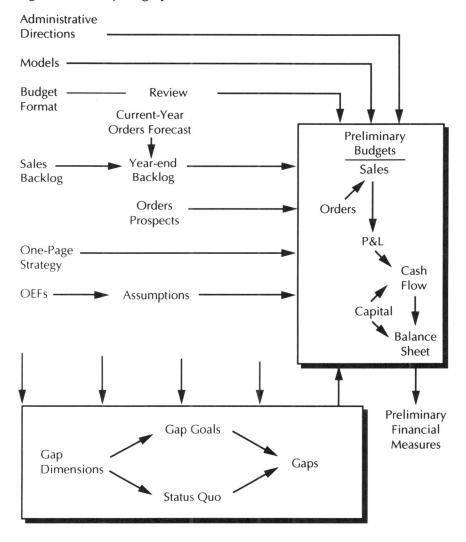

For a multidivision company, this is equivalent to the process for one division. The additional work needed for a multidivision company is discussed in a later section.

The recommended budgeting process consists of two stages. In the early stage, the job is "thinking it through." The output is a preliminary budget that serves two purposes: It is a deliberate checkpoint for examining whether the decisions made and alternatives chosen will yield a satisfactory budget, and it provides direction for the detailed work of the final stage. In the final stage, the work is "crunching the numbers," generating all the detail needed for a useful budget.

What exactly does *preliminary budget* mean in the sense used here? It means a set of broad predictions of the next year's financial performance derived mostly from models, or at least modeling-type thinking. As opposed to the detailed, bottom-up numerical construction of the final budget, its inputs are mostly top-down initial estimates of orders, sales, capital needs, improvement goals, and outside environment behavior. Its goal should be precision of the profit estimate within about 10 percent of the final budget. The key to getting a useful preliminary budget without prohibitive effort is modeling plus, as usual, knowledgeable and competent managers.

Sales for the preliminary budget are predicted on the basis of sales backlog, expected new orders for the current year, and orders prospects for the coming year. Expense and cash flow relations to sales are then used to derive profit and loss and cash flow predictions, for example, "Product line X is expected to have a 35 percent contribution margin," or "Corporate fixed expense should increase 4 percent next year."

This two-stage approach is fundamental to both the effectiveness and efficiency of the final budget as a powerful planning and management tool. If detailed number crunching is done early in the process, it almost certainly will have to be done over, perhaps a number of times. This adds to the amount of work, the frustration, and the confusion of budgeting. Also, management will not know its prospects for the next year until late in the process; changing the budget then involves a lot of rework, done under time pressure. On the other hand, if the first stage of the process involves mainly thinking, with numbers generated only to the extent of models and broad estimates, an unsatisfactory result can be manipulated much more easily into an acceptable budget.

It is difficult to get broad estimates from some managers. Some will do all the details and crunch all the numbers even if told not to do so, because they are just not comfortable making broad estimates. The best way to get useful preliminary numbers is to develop and use business return on investment (ROI) models, as discussed in Chapter 10. Together with the early-stage inputs, a business model can both generate the needed preliminary budget and provide the best vehicle available for analyzing alternative courses of action.

In addition to the *gaps* discussed in the preceding section, the outputs of the early stage are a *preliminary budget* and *preliminary financial measures*. The preliminary budget numbers are based on the assumptions, the preliminary sales forecast for next year, and ideally a business model that relates profit to sales.

Financial measures are the financial parameters against which the company has decided to measure itself; they vary from industry to industry. Typically, ROI, return on equity, and return on capital are financial measures. Things such as days receivables and days inventory may be. Particularly for companies in industries for which extensive statistics are published, various operating and balance sheet ratios may be included for comparison with competition. The numerical values of the selected financial measures, together with comparison to past and present results, largely define a "satisfactory" budget, so these measures should be computed and analyzed as one of the early-stage outputs.

The second or final stage is detailed development of the numbers for the final budget. That final budget and the associated values of the financial measures are the final outputs of the budgeting process.

In addition to the final review and approval by the board of directors, there are two other points at which the approval of the board should be obtained. First, it should approve the strategy, the OEFs, and the assumptions. As noted in Chapter 8, determining the OEFs and the assumptions is an area where the directors can and should make one of their best contributions to the company. Also, the board is the disinterested review body necessary to make the assumptions process work properly, so it should be involved with the initial development of assumptions. Second, the board should approve the preliminary budget. An unsatisfactory prospective budget is more easily changed by management at this point than after detailing all the numbers, and board dissatisfaction addressed at the preliminary budget point will make the final review better and easier.

Process Timing

Because each company must tailor the budgeting process to its specific needs, it is impossible to prepare a definitive schedule that will fit all companies. Even with the best of processes, a large organization must take longer than a small one, because more organization levels must be coordinated, integrated, and consolidated. Some useful general comments can be made, however. The budgeting process should be scheduled backward from the end, with each activity and milestone set as late as possible. This should be done so that the information in the final budget is as fresh as possible, and also so that the organization spends no more time or work on budgeting than is necessary.

For a calendar-year budget, the final review and approval by the board of directors should be scheduled as late in December as practical. Moving backward, some time must be allowed between the president's approval and the board review for final consolidation and presentation in financial format by accounting. With current computer technology, this should take relatively little time.

Scheduling for the final stage must include time for developing gap analysis action programs (some of which will have been done earlier), generating all the numbers, coordinating and reconciling functions, and reviewing and revising at all organizational levels. Tight time pressure is recommended for the final stage. It is here that the process can bog down in details, in part because of the tendency to keep working until somehow certainty is achieved (impossible, of course). The final-stage detailing is one of those activities that will take a month if the people involved are given a month, but the result will be no better than if only one week is allowed.

The goal should be to complete the early stage no earlier than mid-October for a calendar-year budget. The beginning date depends on the nature of the company's strategic planning process. As previously mentioned, a thorough strategic planning process can sharply reduce the time required for the first stage. The early-stage beginning date is also not critical; identifying OEFs and gap dimensions, for example, can be done almost any time. A reasonable goal for most companies is to start the early stage around September 1. The time required to go through the process is more a function of the number of organizational levels than of the number of organizations.

The Process: Early Stage

The early stage is further detailed in Figure 2. It essentially consists of five different types of "thinking it through" activities.

1. *Reviewing the budget format.* The principles and techniques presented in Chapter 9 are used to design a format that provides the information most useful to managers. If the budget has previously been in an accounting format, this will be a major task annually until a sufficiently useful format is achieved. Once a useful format has been obtained, reviewing it will be a minor task, dealing only with changes in the business and desired improvements.

2. *Making a preliminary prediction of the next year's sales.* Since sales are the driving force of all business operations, they must be predicted before expense and capital. There are two sources of the sales prediction: sales backlog and expected new orders. The pertinent sales backlog is that on hand on December 31. Since the preliminary sales prediction will probably be made in September, a prediction must be made of orders that will be received, and not filled, in the remainder of the current year. Current backlog plus this latter forecast equals year-end sales backlog.

The other input to preliminary sales is orders prospects for the next year. As discussed in Chapter 10, forecasting orders and sales is the biggest area of uncertainty in budgeting. Proper use must be made of data, questioned trends, and models. There is also an input from assumptions into the prediction of orders and sales. The result, then, of predicting orders prospects and the effects of assumptions is the preliminary orders budget. The combination of predicted year-end sales backlog plus the preliminary orders budget yields the preliminary sales budget.

This preliminary sales budget should be fairly definitive. Since the proper way to develop it is largely through models, the only way it should change in the final stage is through the introduction of later data of two types: orders obtained in the current year yet unfilled, and orders prospects for the early portion of the next year—the part of the year for which data are the proper forecasting tool. The goal is to predict next year's sales, largely through models and trends, early enough to drive the detailing of expense and capital budgets. Then, as late as possible, subsequent information is added to obtain the final sales budget.

For the type of business in which orders have no meaning, the preliminary sales budget would be developed by modeling the next year with the pertinent assumptions that have been made.

3. *Applying strategic inputs,* including generating assumptions and ensuring consistency of the budget with strategy, is the third type of early-stage budget activity. Assumptions are made for each identified OEF. The one-page strategy statement is reflected in the development of the preliminary budget.

4. *Conducting gap analyses.* Gap dimensions come from many sources and can be identified at any time. Most of those chosen should be known before the budgeting process begins, but early-stage budgeting activity should identify some more. The early-stage gap analysis should define the gaps themselves. This involves defining the next-year goals for the selected gap dimensions and predicting status quo expectations. These tasks are explained in Chapter 11.

5. *Generating the preliminary budgets and financial measures.* The budgets to be generated are orders, sales, profit and loss, capital, cash flow, and the balance sheet. Although all these budgets can be generated simultaneously on a computer, conceptually there is a clear sequence to their preparation, as indicated in Figure 2. Note that no preliminary expense budget is prescribed. Expense

should be generated from a model, with expense budgeting only done in the final stage, because it is essentially detailed number crunching.

The preliminary P&L budget should factor in the results of gap analysis to date. Since, in the early stage, gap action programs will not have yet been defined, there will be an uncertainty as to whether the goals that exist at the time can be met. This is a possible subject for alternative analysis but is essentially a judgment call for the preliminary budget.

The preliminary capital budget does not proceed directly from the others. Since there are usually more perceived capital needs than financial resources to devote to them, the preliminary capital budget input may be as simple as the upper limit the company feels it can afford. Additional inputs to capital budgeting may include the strategy (areas of emphasis), the sales prediction (capacity), gap analysis (action programs to close gaps), and possibly OEFs and assumptions (e.g., competitor quality improvements and new government safety regulations).

The preliminary cash flow and balance sheet budgets are generated last, because their inputs include the P&L and capital preliminary budgets. Their other inputs are assumptions concerning receivables time and the like.

The early stage outputs, the preliminary budget and financial measures, together with the associated thought processes and information, provide a good platform for streamlined preparation of the detailed final budgets. Except for all the iteration and communication involved in both stages, the early stage can be thought of as top-down and the final stage as bottom-up.

The Process: Final Stage

The final stage, shown in Figure 3, is where the details are generated and final budgets prepared. In addition to the administrative directions, models, and budget format, its inputs are the preliminary budget and the identified gaps. The final stage can also be characterized by five different types of activities.

1. *Updating the preliminary orders and sales budgets.* Updating the final numbers for the preliminary orders and sales budgets

Figure 3.   Final-stage process.

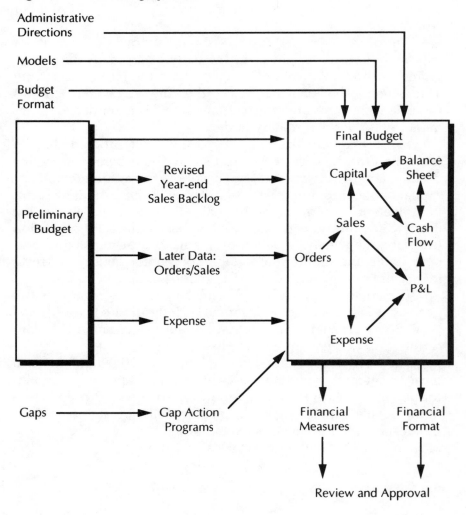

can generally be done simply by using later data, but sometimes a particular event will have changed a conclusion about a trend or an outside influence. In any case, a couple of months will have passed since preparation of preliminary budgets, and they should be modified to include the latest information available. The year-end sales backlog prediction will have to be revised for later in-hand orders and other sales information. The final orders budget is the preliminary orders budget modified by later data on orders prospects. The final sales budget is then derived from the modified year-end backlog prediction plus the final orders budget.

2. *Predicting all company expense.* All costs for the year must be predicted, taking into account the updated sales budget. The work of estimating, reviewing, modifying, and consolidating expense is where most of the dog work of budgeting is done and where most of the psychological games are played. It is also the place where every participant gets involved. A good preliminary budget should reduce both work and frustration. Reviews should center objectively around deviations from models and experience, rather than emotion and psychology. The prediction of costs is discussed in Chapter 10.

3. *Developing action programs to fill the identified gaps.* This is the focal point for encouraging excellence and so must be a major final-stage activity. Developing programs to fill the identified gaps is where specific action planning is done. This is worthy of management's primary attention.

These gap action programs must be specific in content, timing, and resources required. Many gap action programs will contribute only to expense budgeting, but others can offer input to each type of budget (e.g., programs directed at increasing orders or programs directed at improving collections and thus cash flow).

4. *Generating the final budget.* The sequence is similar to that for the early-stage preliminary budget preparation. Here, however, an expense budget is an added element. The final budget must have actual expense estimates, made by the knowledgeable and responsible manager, in sufficient detail for management and control. The P&L budget is derived in this case from both sales and expense budgets.

5. *Reviewing and approving the budget*. The recommended budget should be assembled in the form most useful for management. Accounting must transform the submitted budget into a financial format consistent with generally accepted accounting principles for public reporting and for its lenders. In its review and approval process, the board of directors should study both the management and the financial forms.

The Multidivision Company Process

The easy way for a multidivision company to budget is for the president and the corporate staff to sit back and wait for the division budgets to come in, then review, react, and scream. This says, in effect, that the company is just the sum of its divisional parts. If that is true, at some point the board of directors or owner(s) will conclude that the expensive corporate superstructure is not contributing anything; it will be eliminated, and the divisions will be sold or spun off.

The company president must exert a strong influence on the divisions so that they pursue the desired objectives. But every president faces the dilemma of how much to get involved in division affairs. A hands-off attitude will not achieve what the president wants, unless he or she is lucky. However, if the president dips into the details, division management will be bypassed and rendered ineffective. Division management is there in the first place because the president concluded that the divisions constitute discrete businesses, for each of which a specific focus of management knowledge and direction is needed for best performance. The budget is both a proper and an excellent vehicle to put reality and meaning into the president's overall direction of the company without intruding into the day-to-day management of the divisions. (In particular, the assumptions process for a division is a good way for a president to exert his or her influence.) Therefore, the corporate contribution to multidivision company budgeting must be well and deliberately designed.

Multidivision companies take many forms. At one extreme is the large conglomerate, in which the divisions are both unrelated and autonomous. In such a company, corporate-level strategic and budgeting activity is similar to that of an investment company, rather than that of an operating business. At the other extreme is the small company with closely related and interacting divisions, with one central finance organization. Such a company has one integrated process, the president leads the strategic planning of the company and each division, and the division budgets are interrelated. There are many variations between these extremes.

In any multidivision company, the proper budgeting activities are the same as those presented in Figures 1 through 3, with all the divisions proceeding at the same time. However, any such company must add time and effort to the process to incorporate strategy development, preliminary budget review, and final budget review of the different divisions. Also, if there is extensive interaction among divisions, procedures must be instituted for timely and effective coordination among them.

The Conglomerate With Unrelated, Autonomous Divisions

The conglomerate with unrelated, autonomous divisions will require the least corporate-level activity. The president should guide the assumptions process for the divisions so that the best intelligence is brought to bear and so that the divisions will be consistent on generally applicable subjects. It would be silly, for example, for one division to assume an increased government defense budget for the next year while another assumes a large decrease. (On the other hand, it may be quite proper for one division to assume an increase in defense spending related to its products, while another division assumes a decrease in its particular defense market. Assumptions must be specific.) The assumptions process will clearly benefit from different points of view. Therefore, a conglomerate should add an early process element for development of OEFs and assumptions, and a process for coordination among divisions as they develop their assumptions.

The conglomerate president should also provide the divisions with the one-page strategy statement, even if it is investment strategy rather than operating business strategy, before the development of the divisional one-page strategy statements.

The conglomerate should have corporate-level review of the

preliminary budgets for the same reason it is held in the company with a single business: The direction and emphasis of the budget is much easier to change at that stage if unsatisfactory. Corporate-level review of the final budgets is required, of course. Coordination among divisions during budget preparation will be minimal if the divisions are unrelated, probably limited to presentation formats and financial assumptions, which can be handled among division and corporate financial people.

The Small Company With Closely Interrelated Divisions and One Centralized Finance Organization

In a small company with closely interrelated divisions, the divisional processes will almost blend into a single company process. Companies may have different divisions because they operate in different markets with different products. If those products or markets are all related, such a company should have an integrated total strategy. And although its first concern should be the success of its different divisions, it will look for synergy among them wherever possible. In this case the company strategy will be operational, not just investment. Company and division strategic planning should be integrated into one process, with the company president actively directing it. OEFs and assumptions should still be different for different divisions, but should be related, and their development should be closely coordinated. The president should be actively involved in the "thinking it through" work in the early stage of budgeting, and the early stage should yield a coordinated and integrated result. In the final stage, the divisions should develop their numbers individually but coordinate interrelated work activity.

The biggest mechanical problem in multidivision budgeting is transfer pricing, that is, how to charge products and services "sold" from one division to another within the same company. This is a long-standing subject about which much has been written, so space is not devoted here to the various techniques. There is an important philosophical point, however: Policy should be deliberately decided by the president and his or her top management team. Transfer pricing policy should not just be allowed to evolve through lower-level experts. Generally, a president will not want one division to subsidize another; if a division is noncompetitive, he or she will want to know it. The president may favor competitive transfer pricing, together with a policy that the divisions can buy competitive products and services outside the company if they choose. On the other hand, if a deliberate decision has been made that Division A will build production capability for widgets sufficient to meet total company needs, the president does not want Divisions B, C, and D to buy widgets somewhere else. In this case, the weapon for carrying out this decision is favorable transfer pricing (plus ensuring through good management that Division A makes high-quality widgets, of course). The policy that will *not* work is transfer pricing that allows a division to be noncompetitive but does not allow other divisions to buy outside the company.

The Details

The final step in ensuring good budgeting process flow is to organize the details. This is where the first objective—an accurate, realistic, and consistent budget—is met. The details must also ensure that the objectives of communicating strategy to the organization and developing operating plans across functions are met. Thus, accuracy and consistency of numbers and effective communication are the primary concerns here.

Ensuring Accuracy

First, consider the numbers themselves. There is a large potential for error and confusion inherent in the mass of numbers and the amount of revisions that must be made. Not crunching numbers until the final stage helps, but more must be done. Two ways to reduce the potential for error are to make the number crunching as automatic as possible and to assign specific responsibility and procedures for keeping a strict trail of revisions.

The development and improvement of personal computer spreadsheets over the last decade have been of enormous benefit in number-crunching tasks. All companies should at least distribute spreadsheet-formatted diskettes, rather than paper forms, to all participants for budget input. The system and software should be set up to automatically accept and process these input diskettes. If the company has its personal computers networked, the diskette step can be replaced by direct electronic input. However, the diskette input is the *minimum* that companies should have, because this eliminates one or more error-prone steps of data transcription.

There are various budgeting software packages and modules of larger software systems available. To make information most useful for management, most companies will want to do some customizing of standard packages, so one should be selected with ease of customizing in mind. Fortunately, state-of-the-art spreadsheet software makes it relatively easy for a company to program its own budget system into a spreadsheet. Since most purchased packages will have to be modified anyway, self-generated, spreadsheet-based budget software is often a good alternative.

With automatic data input, it is imperative to design the system so that the inputs flow automatically to wherever they are used, thus eliminating another source of transformation error and inconsistency. For example, an orders input from a particular sales department may be used in, say, six places in the budget. It should be manually input only once and transferred to the other five places by the spreadsheet program. The alternative of six manual inputs cries for error and inconsistency: At some revision in the process, the inputter will forget to make the change at one or more places in the budget. This requirement is obvious to technically trained people, but experience has shown that it is not obvious to all people who design spreadsheets. And even technically trained people sometimes do not properly interconnect a new module added to an existing software system. Similarly, numbers calculated in the program should never be brought out for later manual input; they should flow automatically to wherever they are needed.

The second recommendation for avoiding numerical errors and inconsistencies is to design procedures for maintaining a trail of all budget revisions and to clearly assign responsibility for that task. The appropriate "keeper of the trail" is ordinarily the budget analyst from accounting who is assigned to a particular budget. Spreadsheet software again helps, but the key is to mark each input and output with its revision number and to keep track of these. Positive control should be set up so that the analyst knows every time new data are input (again, this can be partly automatic), and participants should not accept budget outputs from anyone but this same analyst. Procedures should specify that revised inputs not dribble in at random but be held until a certain date or certain event for input of major revisions.

Facilitating Communication

Every function needs to know every way in which other functions affect its work. A function needs to know what is expected of it by management, what the demands on it from other functions are, and what support it should get from other parts of the organization.

The two main communication concerns in budgeting are that every necessary interaction among different organizations be covered consistently and that all elements of cost for a given activity be included; the budget analyst is the proper person to promote and facilitate such communication. Regarding the first concern, familiar activities lend themselves to checklists, and procedures for coordination and multiple sign-offs. For the new or changed activities, the analyst as well as the managers involved must be active and aggressive in identifying contribution and coordination needs. The budget analyst is the key individual to ensure that all elements of cost for a given activity are included. Operating people commonly estimate effort—labor hours, machine hours, direct material, and so on—for an activity and rely on accounting to convert these into correct dollar amounts. Accounting also usually ensures that correct numbers are included for peripheral costs, such as space charges and rent. Accounting people in general, and the budget analyst in particular, are thus the people who should have the best knowledge of all the types of costs incurred in a given activity.

The Budget Analyst

Clearly, the position of budget analyst is an important one. With its mass of numbers and multiple revisions, budgeting is a complex process. It is strongly recommended that a single person, the budget analyst, be empowered to coordinate and expedite the process and to serve as the main "realism and consistency" advisor to management. The budget analyst serves simultaneously as an auditor and a helper and should be chosen, trained, and managed with care. He or she should be a professional and experienced accountant, a well-organized grappler with detail, and a person able to gain the respect and confidence of operating managers while also auditing them. If staffed and empowered correctly, the budget analyst will make a large contribution to a good budget and also serve as a principal financial analyst and advisor throughout the year.

Supplementary Information

Another problem associated with budget details is the tendency of managers, accounting, and planning people to request a volume of supplementary information to help them evaluate budgets. These are often various operating ratios for historical and competitive comparison. The kind of information requested is properly a function of both the type of business and the management style—different managers like to look at different relationships. The volume of this supplementary information often grows and grows as management adds new things of interest but does not delete old information, even though nobody remembers why it was collected in the first place. The annual budget format review should include a "sunset" review of all the supplementary information required. Management should get every bit of such information it feels it needs, but not one bit more, because generating that information takes work.

Administrative Directions

Administrative directions should be the responsibility of accounting, specifically the budget analyst. There may be multiple administrative directions; a multidivision company may have one from the corporate level, one for each division, and perhaps a few within divisions.

The administrative directions should contain all the detailed information needed by the participants to complete their budgets or indicate when that information will be available. The specific content and amount of detail needed will vary from company to company but should always include the following types of information:

- *Schedule.* These directions should be in input/output form and cover at least all the items in Figures 1 through 3 for all levels of participants. For example, "All departmental budgets to division accounting—October 25."

- *Formats and media.* For the early stage, these directions should generally specify document formats where necessary. For the final stage, the completely detailed specifications for submitting figures must be included: numerical formats, medium, and input method. For example, "Use diskette BUDGET1 supplied by accounting September 15, completed diskette to be delivered to accounting by November 5."

- *Preparation, coordination, review, and approval responsibilities.* For example, "Space charges will be prepared by facilities and presented to all departments for review by November 1. Disagreements will be resolved and space charges made final by November 15, by the decision of the executive vice-president if department heads and facilities cannot agree."

- *Assumptions.* All those available should be included, and those not yet available scheduled. Particularly, assumptions from accounting and other corporate staff functions that are needed in operating calculations (e.g., average pay raise, interest rates, foreign currency conversion rates) should be included. If preliminary, a schedule date for final assumptions should be given.

Following are four important miscellaneous points about "the details":

1. The few-but-large-sales business should budget by quarter rather than by month (and then use quarterly plans to predict by month for one quarter at a time). Predictive information for a whole year is not accurate for particular months in such a business.

2. Most companies have a confidentiality versus communication concern; widespread communication is so important to good budgeting that this conflict should be resolved on the side of communications whenever possible.

3. Whenever major changes are made in the budgeting process, extensive orientation for all affected participants should be conducted by management and accounting.

4. All designers of budgeting processes should be aware that the law of diminishing returns applies. Budgeting involves a lot of work, and there is a tendency to increase the work over time in search of better budgets. More work will not make the future less uncertain. In every company's budget preparation, there is a point beyond which the company will be mainly spinning its wheels. The way to get better budgets is to use the process recommended here, not work more on particular elements. Experience and knowledge will make this point of diminishing returns evident to competent managers. The activities of budgeting should be carefully scheduled so that they are cut off before the wheel-spinning stage; managers have other important things to do.

Toward a Powerful Budgeting Process

In implementing a powerful budgeting process, everything cannot be done overnight. While adopting the entire process would be of greatest benefit, value will be obtained from implementing any one of the recommended techniques. The president or division general manager may decide that other problems or opportunities are more important than tackling the whole problem of budgeting all at once. In that case, Chapters 7 through 11 offer possible incremental budgeting improvements and solutions to common problems. Any of the techniques discussed can be implemented independently of the others and can be used to good effect. Similarly, the budgeting and performance of any function will benefit from implementation of any of these techniques, even if the division or company is doing nothing about budgeting.

The difficulty or ease of implementing the recommended

techniques partly depends on the culture and sophistication of the organization. However, some techniques are usually easy to implement, including flexible budgeting, spreadsheets, and business modeling. Some techniques are usually difficult, such as the assumptions process, activity-based costing, and the strategy/budget continuum. The difficulty is related to the degree of change and the different way of thinking that is required.

Some techniques lend themselves to partial implementation and experimentation, including activity-based costing, gap analysis, and modeling.

The value obtained from one technique vis-à-vis another also depends on the problems, strengths, and weaknesses of a company, but some general rules apply. The greatest benefit for strategic management will come from the assumptions process (remember that the commitment and involvement of the board of directors is a requirement, while the other techniques can generally be implemented by management). The greatest operating and problem-solving benefit will come from gap analysis. Selecting the best format and gap analysis will give the greatest benefits in focusing on the most important problems and on the critical factors for success. The greatest benefit in reducing wasted effort will come from automation: spreadsheet and computer network development.

If all things are equal, the easier things should be done first: format determined, spreadsheets designed, and data, questioned trends, and models properly incorporated. Simultaneously or shortly thereafter, experiments in gap analysis and activity-based costing should be conducted in parts of the organization. Depending on the state of strategic planning, the assumptions process and the strategy/budget continuum may be more difficult and take longer to implement. Management may wish to defer these until the other improvements take hold.

The best approach, which will yield the most benefit in the least time, is the most aggressive. With the necessary approval of the board of directors, top management announces to the organization the decision to undertake a three-year program to replace budgeting pain with power. Given specific company needs, problems, strengths, and weaknesses, management decides where it wants the company to be in three years, at the end of the program. It then lays out the tasks and timing to accomplish the program, including phases of experimentation, partial implementation, and partial results. Modifications in goals and tasks as the program progresses must be expected: The organization will be learning intensively, and some needs and problems will change. If the program is properly designed and presented, the short-term result will be a better-motivated organization that appreciates that management is firmly addressing one of its continuing frustrations. The long-term result will be powerful budgeting and better company performance.

FUNCTIONAL MANAGERS: SURMOUNTING A POOR BUDGETING PROCESS

Chapters 6 through 11 discuss how a functional manager caught in a poor budgeting process can improve his or her own budgeting and that of other parts of the company. Such improvements will help the functional manager be more satisfied, manage better, and be less vulnerable to the irrationality of poor budgeting.

To accomplish such improvements in the midst of a poor budgeting process, a functional manager needs a logical private process that will generate the needed information and be timely relative to the company's budgeting process. He or she must start the work early because much of the work will be "spare time" activity; the function's work must get done every day, and this private budgeting work will not have been sanctioned by anybody.

The functional manager should do three things before the company's budgeting process begins. Fortunately, major effort in each is needed only once; in succeeding years they will only need to be reviewed and checked.

1. Define the function's activities, inputs, outputs, and cost drivers.
2. Define the important OEFs and internal uncontrollable factors (IUFs) (see the last section of Chapter 8) pertinent to the function. It would be well to make tentative assumptions regarding them, to be finalized during the company's budgeting process.
3. Decide the private budget format. This format follows from the cost drivers, and also from the problems on which the manager wants to focus.

The sequence is important. An inside-out process is the best way to generate OEFs and IUFs. This means reasoning from organization inputs and outputs to the applicable OEFs and IUFs, rather than starting with the latter. OEFs will probably be an unfamiliar concept to a functional manager's key people and possibly difficult to grasp. If the functional manager begins with consideration of OEFs, he or she may never get to useful answers.

Other appropriate preliminary activity is to define the dimension for gap analysis that the function will focus on for the next year's budget. This can be done any time but should be cut off early in the company's budgeting process so that plans are not being changed while numbers are being generated. Since the gap analysis dimension can affect the private-budget format desired, it would be best for that dimension to be defined before the format is decided on in the above sequence.

With this preliminary work done, the functional manager will know the inputs needed when the company's budgeting process begins. He or she can then concentrate on getting any missing inputs. When the needed inputs become available, it is time to make the final assumptions on which the budget will be based.

The important scheduling concern is to finish the preliminary work before the company's budgeting process begins, which might dictate that the preliminary work be started at least two months prior to budgeting. A characteristic of poor budgeting processes is time pressure on the functional managers. Once budgeting begins, the functional manager will be overwhelmed by urgent number crunching; he or she must have done the "thinking it through" earlier.

The functional manager should try to steer all budget reviews toward the meaningful terms of the private process. He or she should explain his or her budgeting rationale in terms of activities, inputs, outputs, cost drivers, OEFs, IUFs, and assumptions. He or she should emphasize the important parameters and their relationships, while also paying attention to the parameters tracked by the company's budgeting system. The functional manager should justify numbers in terms of data, questioned trends, and models. Finally, he or she should use the gap analysis framework to explain problems, goals, and planned actions.

The functional manager should then try to guide the superior's reactions to his or her budget in the same terms. The budget submission should be defended in those terms. If the superior wants numbers changed, the functional manager should try to get the superior to put the desired change in terms of a changed assumption. He or she must respect a superior's emphasis on the parameters that the system tracks but should seek increased emphasis on the parameters he or she believes most important. The functional manager should also seek to put the discussion in terms of models where appropriate, rather than data or trends.

13

Conclusion: Benefits of Powerful Budgeting

Throughout this book, examples show a number of specific business benefits from good budgeting: aid in downsizing, in assimilating a new acquisition, in showing the need for strategy changes, in solving interfunction problems, in providing information for better pricing, and in valuation of a division. The book also gives many additional examples of how a powerful budgeting process can help functional managers to manage better. Such benefits are not normally associated with budgeting, but the examples illustrate the potential when budgeting is taken seriously as a planning and management tool.

Owners first want the company to survive; then they want it to be made more valuable. Management characteristics needed to achieve both goals include good decision-making skills, excellence in all activities, control of all activities, and intelligent and timely reaction to problems and surprises. Good budgeting provides the information, focus, and attitudes needed for each.

The biggest difficulties for most company managers in both surviving and making their companies more valuable are the uncertainty of the future and the uncontrollability of outside environmental factors. Particularly important, major problems come from unpredicted change in the outside environment, ranging from the 1970s oil shocks on a global basis to the sudden defection of a major customer on a local basis. Reacting well in a timely fashion to unpredicted outside events is almost the definition of good management, and this is probably the area in which good budgeting can make its greatest contribution to better business results.

All too often in business, budgeting is deadening and demotivating, the place where vision and inspiration are killed by a bureaucratic exercise that seems uncoupled from the objectives and strategies preached by top management. Budgeting should be uplifting, challenging, and exciting. It can be the mechanism that brings the organization together to grapple with opportunities and problems. Even in a negative situation in which survival is in question, the organization can be powerfully motivated by knowing and facing the real problems and planning their solutions. The final business benefit of good budgeting, then, is the better results that follow from increased motivation and morale of the entire company.

Appendix

A New Manager's First Budget

If you are a new manager, congratulations! You have entered a world that presumably you hope to inhabit for a long time. Managers have a large potential for doing good by doing their jobs well. Good budgeting is a tool that will help you do well.

If you have not been exposed to budgeting before, you probably have some of the following questions about the subject: "What do you want from me?" "What is a budget, really?" "How important is it?" This Appendix addresses such concerns of new managers who are unfamiliar with budgeting.

Budgeting is often a daunting task to the uninitiated. In some companies it is approached with a curious mixture of disinterest and awe. "We only have a week to do this, so throw something together so we can get back to interesting work. But, by the way, you will not be allowed to exceed the costs in your budget next year, no matter what happens." Budgeting is a necessary task. Managers live and work in the future, as well as the present. Planning is a major element of any management job. A budget is the numerical expression of the plans for the next year; because it is specific and immediate, it is probably the company's most important plan. Therefore, it is an important management tool.

If you replace the disinterest and awe with knowledge, understanding, and some approaches and techniques, budgeting will not be difficult, and it will be useful. Understanding powerful budgeting, as presented in this book, will give context and purpose to your budgeting work. You should particularly benefit from the sections at the ends of Chapters 6 through 12, entitled

"Functional Managers: Surmounting a Poor Budgeting Process." Beyond that, this Appendix addresses fundamental subjects to get a new manager started: what budgeting is, planning, budget forms, activities and outputs, costs and cost estimating, and use of computers.

Do not expect a cookbook solution for filling out your budgeting forms. Each function and each budget is different, and only the manager in place has the knowledge to complete his or her budget. But the principles, approaches, and techniques that follow will help.

What Is This Thing Called Budgeting?

In a nutshell, here are the concepts a new manager should keep in mind as he or she approaches the first budget:

- *The budget is the company's statement of expected financial results for next year.* The new manager's portion of the budget is a statement, first, of his or her department's expected costs. (The new manager might be expected to express these in terms of effort— man-hours—and unit purchases, to be converted into dollars by accounting people.) If appropriate, the new manager's budget will also include function outputs—orders, sales, units assembled, and so forth. All this information will generally be required by quarter or by month. A wide variety of supplementary and supporting information might also be required: manpower loading, use of particular services, assumptions, and so on.

- *The purpose of the budget is to give meaning to the company's objectives and priorities by* planning *next year's work in detail and to coordinate and communicate those plans throughout the company.* The new manager's role is to *plan* the organization's work, describe the plans and expected results numerically, and coordinate those plans with other functions with which he or she interacts. The manager is also obliged to plan within the context of the company's goals, strategies, and priorities, and to strive continually for excellence and improved performance.

If the company does not have a good budgeting process, the new manager may get little guidance on his or her first budget.

Forms or a diskette may arrive on his or her desk with no notice, together with a memo from the budget analyst giving a few ground rules and stating that the numbers are due back in about a week. The new manager's boss, when approached, may say little more than "forecast what you think all the costs will be for the next year, fill out the forms, and then we will discuss it."

It would be a mistake to assume, because of such a casual approach, that the company believes the budget is unimportant. In some companies, there is an absolute prohibition against overspending a budget. In most companies, a missed budget will be taken seriously, requiring corrective action, or at least the manager involved will lose image and credibility. In a few companies, the budget truly is not important; however, even there, managers who miss budgets are handy whipping boys or girls if profit problems surface during the year.

- *Each type of business, and indeed each company, has somewhat different costs it wants to accumulate and different groupings of costs.* Thus each company's budget forms tend to be unique, and there is little to be gained from learning generalized budget forms. Rather, the new manager should spend time with his or her budget analyst for an explanation of the particular forms and the company's budgeting process; this should be done before the budgeting process begins. (The term *budget analyst* is used here generically to describe the financial person responsible for integrating budgets. The title may be different in a particular company, but there will be someone with that function.)

- *The budget should be thought of as the numerical expression of the new manager's plans for his or her organization's work for the next year.* The best way to approach it is in terms of required outputs (production, accomplishments, and requirements satisfied) and needed inputs (costs, support required from other functions, and outside purchases). Most important for the new manager to understand are the activities and inputs and outputs that drive costs. Of course, the need for this understanding goes beyond budgeting; it is fundamental to doing the job. As in all cases, good budgeting practice is consistent with good management.

Planning

The words *plan*, *plans*, and *planning* appear frequently in the preceding section. They are the key words in understanding budgeting. The budget is the organization's plan for next year—or, more rigorously, the numerical expression of that plan. Since it is short-term and numerical, it should be specific and detailed.

The ever-uncertain future makes planning more important, not less. A smart person once said, "Plans are nothing, but planning is everything." As conditions change, plans must change. But at any given time, the organization must know what it will be doing today and tomorrow. As conditions change, the current plan must be known in order to intelligently evaluate changes in the plan. Plans must contain enough latitude and contingency to accommodate a reasonable range of uncertainty. In making a plan for serving customers, a manager never knows how many customers will come into the store on a given day in July of next year. However, the plan should accommodate an expected range of customers and possibly include a provision for calling in part-time help to handle a higher peak. The plan itself would not be changed until data over a period of time showed that the general daily level of customers was higher or lower than expected.

A plan is the expression of the way resources—money, people, purchased items—will be used to achieve particular results. It should start with the desired *result*, both in kind and in amount. Then it must state *what* will be done and *how* it will be done. All such *activities* must be scheduled, in terms of start and completion dates. *Assumptions* used in the plan must be stated. Finally, the *cost* and different resources required to carry out the plan must be provided.

The shorter the term of the plan, the more detail it must contain to be useful. A short-term planner should always be able to answer the question, "What are you going to be doing a week from Tuesday?" Planners seldom have complete information about necessary activities when the plan is prepared. In that case, it is both valid and necessary to state that a decision must be made about how to do a particular thing. Then the plan needs a date by which that decision will be made and the nature of activities involved in making the decision.

Too many plans in business seem to be designed to impress the reader with the writer's knowledge of the subject rather than tell the reader what will be *done*. They are long, impressive documents, with erudite discussions of applicable theory and principles, but short on desired results and activities.

Assume that you want to build a house. Your desired result is a certain number of rooms and particular features, plus a desired cost range or maximum. You will not let the builder start your house on the basis of a discussion demonstrating how much he or she knows about houses, plus some general ideas about your house. You will require plans, drawings, schedules, a rendering of the completed house, and cost estimates that will exactly describe the house that will be built for you. You will probably let the builder start before every single decision is made, but you will carefully note what decisions remain and when they must be made to keep the construction on schedule. Keep the house example in mind when you are required to plan or budget anything. It will not be sufficient to impress your superior with what you know; you must convey what you will *do*.

The Process

The new manager's first budgeting task is to fill out the budget forms and submit them. The forms will call for all his or her organization's costs, on a quarterly or monthly basis. Depending on the function, the forms may also require a monthly or quarterly enumeration of organization outputs: units assembled, engineering labor applied to contracts, and so on. The forms may call for textual supplements covering output, support required from other functions, assumptions, and the like.

Some sort of compensation planning is generally done before or during budgeting. This may be as simple as having a ground rule that an *x* percent raise be assumed for all employees on their anniversary dates or as complex as generating an approved prediction of the date and amount of raises for each employee by name. One way or another, planned salary increases must be included in the budgeted personnel costs.

After submission, three things happen, essentially simultaneously. The submission is reviewed by the superior, and the manager is expected to explain, justify, and defend the numbers. There will also be comparisons with the functions with which the organization interacts to check consistency. At the same time, the budget analyst will be operating on the submission, compiling it with those from other departments and adding burden rates and costs and allocated costs.

There undoubtedly will be multiple reviews and iterations of the new manager's budget. After the first review, the superior's budget will be reviewed by the next manager up the line, and so on. Each review may cause changes, which will then have to be reflected back down the organization. This process can take months and be full of surprises for the new manager. For instance, he or she might believe, more than once, that the budget has been approved only to find expenses cut *again* as a result of a higher management review.

The preceding paragraphs suggest some procedures to follow:

1. Keep careful notes of the assumptions, reasoning, and calculations behind the budget submission. Weeks later, when a particular number is attacked in a new review, you may not remember the source of that number.
2. Absent other information about the superior, expect the costs in the first submission to be cut, and understand that the first cut may not be the last. Therefore, do not cut them to the bone in the first submission.
3. If costs are cut beyond your belief of what is required to do the job, make this known to your superior.
4. Use the techniques discussed in Part II to justify the budget, and in particular use gap analysis to identify, attack, and explain problems.

To do the budgeting work intelligently, you should learn a number of things before the budgeting forms arrive on your desk. For example:

- The forms, the process, and your part in it (from the budget analyst)
- The activities and outputs of the organization, and what dictates them
- The elements of cost for activities within your responsibility, the relationships between different costs, and what drives those costs
- The use of a computer to help analyze and prepare the budget

Budget Forms

While there is little use dwelling on the budget forms themselves, because of their uniqueness to each company, a general discussion is appropriate. The highest-level budget forms are those for the entire company and include profit and loss, balance sheet, and cash flow. A P&L budget form for a company might look like the one shown in Figure 4.

In the headings for the P&L form, Q means quarter; this sample budget is done by quarters, rather than months. Sales backlog must be understood as "beginning" or "ending"; if "ending," another column is needed at the beginning of the form for backlog at the beginning of the year. For any quarter, ending backlog equals beginning backlog plus orders minus sales.

The budget form shown in Figure 4 accumulates direct expense and then indirect expense. "Direct other" is commissions, travel charged to customers, and the like. The number and types of indirect expense lines are determined by management's decision concerning the desired visibility of different kinds of costs; they are usually more summarized on the company form than on individual function forms. The budget usually has an "other" category of indirect cost for expenses not itemized.

The new manager's budget form in this company would be derived from the company form but might not look much like it, except for the same columns for quarters or months. Some budget forms do not include descriptions of organization outputs, only costs. For example, a general and administrative function, such as human resources, does not have outputs that are financially

Figure 4. P&L budget form.

	199X Company P&L Budget				
	1st Q	2nd Q	3rd Q	4th Q	Total
Sales backlog					
Orders					
Sales					
Direct expense					
Direct labor					
Direct material					
Direct other					
Total direct expense					
Contribution margin					
Indirect expense					
Indirect labor					
Benefits					
Travel and living					
Advertising					
Indirect material					
Rent					
Utilities					
Outside services					
Other					
Total indirect expense					
Profit from operations					
Other income (expense)					
Profit before tax					
Income taxes					
Net Income					

described. Rather, its outputs are things like benefits administration, training, personnel problem solving, and new hires. Even a direct function like factory assembly may have no place for output on its forms. Its outputs are numbers of units of particular products sent to the test function; those units do not become financially described until they are shipped (thus becoming sales).

Even if such outputs are not on the budget form, it is important that the manager describe, in writing that accompanies the form, the level of output that can be accomplished with the budgeted costs. The new manager must immediately establish the relationship of input and output in his or her proposed budget and work hard to maintain the visibility of that relationship with his or her superior.

Concerning costs, the budget form also predicts personnel costs. For such functions as human resources, and in companies that do not subdivide labor costs, this may require just listing names and salaries and spreading these across the year (remembering to adjust them for planned salary increases). For a factory assembly organization, it would be more complex. The assembly manager would probably have to predict which person would charge direct to which projects; "indirect of direct" for the time direct people charge to such items as training and idle time; or indirect for the manager and secretary. For any manager involved with direct expense, the budget would probably require listing all types of costs, including personnel, by project, usually with a project name and number.

The budget form also lists various nonpersonnel expenses, and the new manager must predict those he or she expects to incur. The human resources manager, for example, may have expenses for travel and living, advertising, office supplies, reference books and magazines, personnel recruiting, and capital outlays for personal computers. The assembly manager may have expenses for indirect material, maintenance, and repair services, and capital expenditures for tools and equipment. Benefits, rent, utilities, and other allocated expenses are normally calculated by financial people.

Activities, Inputs, and Outputs

The best and most fundamental way for you as a new manager to understand your job is in terms of your organization's inputs, activities, and outputs. This is also the best way to prepare for your first budget.

Outputs are the results required from the organization. *Activities* are what the organization does to achieve those outputs. *Inputs* are what are required to carry out the activities. The costs of the organization are determined by all three: what has to be done and how much, how it is done, and what the starting point is. You should explicitly think through the activities, inputs, and outputs of your organization, expressing them in block-diagram or flow-chart form. If you do this before the budgeting process begins, you will have a good head start.

Consider a payroll function in any business. Its outputs are timely paychecks for every employee, in the right amount, with the correct deduction withheld and a record of the pay and all the deductions, and satisfaction or inquiries and complaints. Its inputs are pay and deduction instructions, time records, computer programs and data entry procedures, and general company policies and procedures. Its activities include reviewing and entering time records, reviewing payroll data prepared by the computer, entering changes in salaries and deductions (including periodic changes in applicable tax regulations), correcting errors, making adjustments, and handling inquiries. In common with every function, there is another activity that can be called *administration*—management activities such as training, coaching, communication, and compliance.

The list of activities may seem surprisingly long for something as conceptually simple as a payroll function, and some activities might have been missed. Most functions are required to perform more activities than are recognized intuitively. Some functions have few and obvious outputs, while others have many and more nebulous ones. Outputs vary with responsibility and organization: The ordinary output of a purchasing organization is not a purchase order but receipt of proper material. However, if another organization has responsibility for expediting and receipt, purchasing's output would properly be purchase orders. Similarly, inputs vary with process and procedure, causing activities to vary: Automation of time records would change payroll's input and remove the activity of "entering time records." Your block diagram or flow chart of your organization's activities, inputs, and outputs must be specific to your particular organization.

This discussion also illustrates how intertwined different functions are. Doing things differently in other organizations changes a given function's inputs and outputs and therefore its activities. Most problems are interfunction problems, and most progress is made by finding better ways to do things across functions.

For our purposes, the point is that knowing *all* the activities, inputs, and outputs in a given situation is the only way to fully understand a function, what it does and what it should do, and therefore how much it will cost and what its proper budget should be.

Organization Outputs

There are many types of business organizations with many kinds of outputs and differing degrees of uncertainty in budgeting for them. Few are as simple as "produce *x* widgets." Just as orders and sales are the hardest variables to predict for a company, outputs are the hardest to predict for a functional department. As a new manager, you must understand what dictates your outputs, and this depends on the type of organization you head.

The most prominent dictator of functional outputs is sales. In some organizations, outputs follow directly from sales. Examples are an engineering organization totally devoted to customer development contracts, or a service organization totally devoted to customer maintenance contracts. Other organizations cannot define their output directly from sales but must use something derived from it. Factories generally have a function, perhaps called production control or planning, that schedules all operations. The managers of the assembly, test, and machine shop functions have their outputs defined by planning's schedule, rather than directly by sales.

Then there are functions whose outputs are determined by "structural" factors, independent of sales except in a gross sense. Public financial reporting is one such activity, and structural outputs of accounting are annual and quarterly financial reports. Another example is the requirement for a two-hour response time to a customer service call; that dictates an output for a customer service function, dependent not on sales but on location of customers. Similarly, the work of a security guard function might be defined by the numbers of stations and hours to be covered.

Yet other functions only perform support services for other organizations, e.g., reproduction, word processing, and art departments. These can be called "level of effort" functions, and their output is determined simply by the demand of their "customers," which might be unpredictable in any useful budgeting sense. The customers should be queried on expectations, but defining the output of such "level of effort" functions often comes down to defining a capacity to serve. That is, one starts with cost and then states the capacity which that cost provides. (Sometimes that capacity is dictated by higher management as an arbitrary cost-control mechanism.)

Finally, some functional outputs are dictated by outside environmental factors, the same OEFs that were featured prominently in Part II, or by company business decisions. New kinds of state taxes dictate new outputs from tax accounting. A decision to reorganize may give a particular function a new set of "customers" and different responsibilities. A new product decision may affect the outputs of many functions: engineering, manufacturing, sales, purchasing, contracts, inventory accounting.

In practice, one functional organization may have all these different types of outputs, and perhaps others. Different outputs of purchasing might be dictated by sales, factory schedules, a requirement to service random headquarters needs, inventory policy, or new product decisions.

Starting with these general categories, you need to define your outputs and learn where to get the information needed to specify those outputs for the budget and when that information will be available. If the company's process is so poor that you are expected to submit the budget before the needed information is available, assumptions must be made, labeled as such. Outputs should be expressed in the budget submission, even if partly qualitative and partly based on assumptions. They define the job and indicate what is expected of the organization. Concentrated attention to outputs will be appreciated by your superior, help him or her do the job, and lead to a better budget.

The Elements of Cost

The first thing you need to know about costs is the nature of the costs your organization will incur, plus the way the company groups these costs and the definition of the terms used for them.

Types of Costs

The types of costs in a business fall into a number of natural categories. One way to start is to divide costs into things that the company *makes* or *does* and the things that the company *buys*. Another fundamental classification for many businesses is by costs that directly provide products and services—that is, direct expense—and all other expenses, called indirect expense.

The costs of what the company makes or does are labor costs. Unfortunately for a general discussion such as this, various types of businesses handle labor costs quite differently. For example:

- In some retail businesses and many small businesses, labor costs are simply the salaries of the employees.

- Manufacturing businesses generally wish to keep track of their direct expense to know the profitability of their various products. For that, time spent on (charged to) direct labor on each project or product must be known, and time records are kept of how employees spend and charge their time. Employees are often labeled as direct or indirect. The indirect people—all general and administrative people, managers, engineers, planners, secretaries—charge their time to indirect labor. (Further categorization of their time occurs if the company relates indirect activities to sales through activity-based costing, as discussed in Chapter 10.) The direct people also have idle time, training time, and the like, which gives rise to a category often called "indirect of direct."

- In an engineering organization that works on customer contracts, internally funded product development, and sales proposals, the first two are ordinarily considered direct labor expense, while the last is considered indirect expense. The operative difference is that direct costs are burdened in some way with overhead charges, while indirect costs are not.

• In service companies, labor costs range from simple "labor cost equals salaries" to complete project accounting similar to that for a factory. It depends on the type of service and the way it is billed. Financial service and personal service companies generally follow the simple path.

• Some distribution companies compute cost of sales and gross margin but only include material costs therein. All labor costs are considered, in effect, indirect expense.

For companies that break down labor costs into direct and indirect, the remainder of salary and wage costs—vacations, holidays, sick leave—plus things like insurance that the company buys go into benefits expense.

The grouping and presentation of products or services that a company *buys* are more arbitrary and variable than labor costs. The importance of different "buy" costs varies by business, by management, and over time. For example, office supplies is a minor category for manufacturing businesses and might just be included in the "other indirect" category. However, a word processing bureau would probably budget and track office supplies as a significant expense. If management of any company gets concerned about any expense, chances are it will soon be budgeted and tracked separately to give its control the desired emphasis.

The most important purchases of any business are those directly related to its sales. In retail and distribution businesses, the products sold are generally identical to those bought. The same thing is true of a bank, which primarily buys and sells money. In manufacturing businesses, raw materials, components, and subassemblies are bought and turned into products by labor. In utilities, systems and equipment, fuel and power, and sometimes raw materials are bought and turned into delivered services through labor. For maintenance service businesses, the comparable things bought are tools, spare parts, shop equipment, and perhaps trucks. These various items are called by different names in different businesses; the most common term in manufacturing businesses is direct material.

All companies buy additional products or services to conduct their businesses:

1. *Personnel-related*. These are memberships, subscriptions, travel and living, training courses, and so on. Most of these are related to increasing knowledge and information and thus the skills and value of the work force.
2. *Facilities-related*. These include rent, utilities, maintenance and repair, and security guards. If the facilities are owned, there will be depreciation and amortization rather than rent. Improvements to facilities are usually capital expenditures, whether the facility is owned or leased.
3. *Outside services*. These are consultants, legal expense, design and drafting services, temporary personnel, and the like.

Every business has other costs not included in these categories, e.g., advertising and sales promotion, freight, and taxes. However, these categories give a starting point to learn particular cost elements.

Generally, capital expenditures have to be budgeted separately from expense items. The idea of capital expenditures follows from the accounting principle that costs should be matched with revenue on the P&L statement. Consider a piece of major equipment expected to be used for five years in building products that will generate sales. An erroneous picture of profitability would result from expensing the total cost of the equipment right away—this year's profit would be unrealistically low, while the next four years' would be unrealistically high. Therefore, major expenditures for items expected to have multiyear use are capitalized and depreciated (expensed) over the period of use. There are different acceptable methods of depreciation, but a common one for public accounting is the simple straight-line. If something is expected to have a five-year life, one-fifth of its costs is charged to each of the five years. Typical capital expenditures include factory equipment, tools, computers, test equipment, and improvements to the facility.

Cost Relationships

After you understand the different types of costs, you should become familiar with the relationships among them. For example:

- If there is a given amount of remote work to be done—selling, customer contact, working with project partners—travel and living and telecommunications expense cannot both be reduced. If one cuts travel and living, he or she must expect telecommunications expense to increase.
- To make sense, outside contracting of tasks must reduce labor expense.
- The cost of high-priced professional people necessarily includes costs of things that keep them current in their professions, such as memberships, seminars, courses, and books and magazines. If the business needs these professional people, management must accept that such supporting expenses are simply costs of doing business.
- The usual outcome of new information technology is the ability to do more things, not reduced costs. The proliferation of computers of every kind is a good example. The main effect of widely available facsimile machines has been a greatly increased perception of the number of things that need to be communicated instantaneously. The realistic justification for such new technology is usually better performance rather than lower cost.

Cost Drivers

The third aspect of costs you as a new manager need to know about is what drives them. Cost drivers are discussed in Chapter 9; the concern there is to relate indirect costs to company outputs so as to better know the profitability of different products and to understand how to reduce costs rationally. Here the concern is to understand what drives costs so that you can plan and budget them intelligently.*

---

*The most important use of knowledge of cost drivers is not in budgeting, but in improving performance and reducing costs, i.e., striving for excellence. Procedures and processes and structure are places to look for such improvements

In general, costs are driven by required outputs, procedures and processes used (how activities are done), and by structure. Required outputs refer to function outputs, not overall company sales or profit. Different procedures and processes surely produce different particular costs, and probably overall costs as well. A simple example is that "buying" rather than "making" will reduce labor costs and increase material costs; if the buy decision is correct, it will reduce total costs. Another example is that automating design and drafting work will change both particular and overall costs.

Structure here means not only organizational structure but also the basic realities within which the company conducts its business. Consider two otherwise identical companies, one of which does all its work at one location, while the other has two widely separated locations in different states. Some of the second company's costs will be higher simply because of this "structural" factor of two locations: two receiving and shipping functions, two state tax accounting functions, two guard forces, and so on.

Some cost drivers may seem identical to output dictators previously discussed. For example, is the number of stations that must be covered by a security guard force a structural output dictator or a structural cost driver? The answer is that we do not care. The important thing is that you understand what dictates your outputs and drives your costs, not how to classify each; do not let semantics get in the way of the task at hand.

A range of examples will give guidance concerning where to look for cost drivers (consider taxes to be included in each example).

- In a financial services company, costs tend to be driven by interest rates and securities prices, telecommunications, salary and commission levels, and computing.

- In a factory, direct labor is driven first by sales or schedules derived from sales. It is also driven by processes used, wage lev-

(although structure may be far beyond the new manager's control). But do not rule out "required outputs" as a source of improvement. For example, if a factory assembly function adds a quality output requirement (the "do it right the first time" approach) for products handed over to test, an element of quality work beyond assembly will be eliminated.

els, the degree of automation, skill levels, and structural factors such as the proximity of workers to their inputs. Indirect labor is driven by the engineering, planning, and material content of the work and by process characteristics such as the number of engineering changes that must be handled.

• Engineering costs can be driven by such things as sales, new product decisions, the number of engineering changes needed (driven in turn usually by the maturity of the products), the amount of design and drafting automation, and the availability of computers and software.

• In a retail or distribution business, labor costs can be driven by sales, number and complexity of products sold, hours of operation, wage and salary levels, and possibly the amount of travel required.

• Material costs are driven by product specifications, design characteristics, vendor prices, scale economies, purchasing clout (generally a result of amount purchased and credit standing), location, and industry structure relative to suppliers.

• Each general and administrative expense tends to have its own cost drivers, mostly structural. Accounting costs tend to be driven by size and complexity (for example, how many dissimilar divisions there are) of the company, whether it is public or private, international or local, and so on. Legal costs have a structural everyday-business level beyond which they depend strongly (and alarmingly) on the litigiousness of the company's environment.

Cost Estimating

The fourth and final thing you need to know about costs is how to estimate or predict them. The tenets of Chapter 10 apply. The first principle concerns the proper use of data, trends, and models. The second is to base cost predictions on firm understanding of organization outputs, cost drivers, and the relationships between them. Here the concern is more basic: to help the new manager grasp the fundamental concepts of cost estimating.

Budget costs are aggregates of many activity and element costs. The first step is, again, planning—deciding the work to be done and the purchases that must be made. Individual item costs must then be predicted, properly summed, and spread over time to get budget costs. All activities should be divided into things to be *done* or *made* and things to be *bought*.

For things *bought*, the simplest costs to estimate are for items or services for which the price and quantity are known, e.g., a magazine subscription. Unfortunately, few costs are this easy to estimate. Known forthcoming price changes are also simple to estimate. Expected or possible price changes require judgment, which should be supported by the best information obtainable about future prices.

Next in simplicity to estimate are costs of purchases for which firm quotations are in hand. Firm quotations from suppliers are the only fully accurate way to cost purchases for new products or activities.

Then there are known items whose quantity and price will vary, such as food for a restaurant. The restaurant buyer knows the food well, but prices vary frequently, and the amount needed will depend on sales, which must be estimated. The estimates must be based on knowledge, experience, assumptions, plans, data, trends, and models, as appropriate. The manager responsible for buying food must use budgeted sales (done by someone else) plus a set of outside factors (those that influence food prices locally) and restaurant actions (quality of food, buying quantities, substitution of ingredients) to predict food costs for next year. (The annual budget, of course, can present fairly broad estimates. The detailed, precise planning for a restaurant will probably be done on a weekly basis.)

Finally, there are new purchases that will have to be made, but the kinds or quantities are not yet well enough known to get firm quotations. Such cost predictions must be derived from broad estimates from suppliers, from knowledge of similar purchases in the past, or from general knowledge. New products, planned but yet to be designed, are usually in this category.

For things *done* or *made*, part of cost estimating is easy, part difficult. The easy part is predicting salaries and wages of the people involved. These are either known or can be closely estimated. The effort required to do repetitive tasks that have been done before is also easy; man-hours of effort times salaries (or direct labor rates), both known data, is the cost. The hard part is predicting the effort required to do new tasks, or old tasks in new ways, or new projects. These must be estimated from knowledge and experience from similar work. If no one has such direct knowledge and experience, the new project or task must be broken into elements to which knowledge and experience can be applied.

In short, the best information available about purchase prices and work effort must go into cost prediction. Direct experience, known prices, and firm quotations are best. If none of these are possible, go to whatever source gets closest to one of them.

There is no magic way to do cost estimation well. As mentioned in Chapter 10, there are no general algorithms that tell an engineering manager how much it will cost to design a product. Good cost predictions ultimately depend on the knowledge, intelligence, and experience of the managers involved.

Using Computers

Here the subject is not budgeting software; that is for accounting, management information systems, and top management to consider. Rather, the subject is how using a computer can help the new manager in budgeting. In most cases the appropriate tool is one of the various spreadsheet programs, readily available and easy to use. You are probably already computer-literate; if not, you should begin to learn. Needed are small, simple spreadsheet programs on a personal computer to analyze work, outputs, and costs, and these are relatively easy to do even with only a rudimentary knowledge of the computer.

Usually the new manager's first task is to gather data; you probably do not know immediately the specific analysis desired. After deciding the data to track, you can design a spreadsheet, which can be sorted in various ways, on which the data can be captured. A secretary or clerk can keep it updated, or you can do it. As you become more familiar with the job, you will discover useful ways to analyze the data. This calls for simple models (see Chapter 10) that can also be done with the spreadsheet program.

With the data and simple models available on the computer, you can accumulate and analyze costs, relate inputs to output, do "what if" analyses, justify a process or procedural change, and justify capital expenditures. The beauty of using the computer spreadsheet is that it readily captures and holds large amounts and varieties of data, much more than is practical in any manual system. The initial difficulty is knowing which data you will want later. Start by capturing all data of conceivable interest, then weed some out as you learn their relative importance. Otherwise, the data generation becomes an onerous end in itself.

When you start, think about which costs, activities, inputs, and outputs should be captured. At the same time, investigate which programs and information are already available. The company's management information system may already supply the needed information, or much of it. People in MIS, accounting, or other departments may already have spreadsheet programs that will meet your needs. Ideally, use the company system if possible; private systems inevitably differ from the company system because of errors in data entry or other problems, so if you use your own system, you will draw conclusions from different figures than those used by everyone else. The next best thing is to download data from the company system to a personal computer for analysis by a program already developed. Do not duplicate work to develop a program that is already available. If your investigation comes up empty, however, you must design and program the desired spreadsheets or have someone do it for you.

Examples abound of data that can be captured this way to yield useful information to the new manager. A purchasing manager can track all purchase orders, with the ability to sort them by size and by originating function. Engineering and factory planning managers can capture the source and costs of engineering change notices, for later analysis of the process or the trends and payoffs of change notices by product. An engineering manager can keep his or her project manpower plan on a spreadsheet. This plan will probably change as projects are added or canceled, or are perceived to involve more or less work than originally thought; the spreadsheet makes it easy to analyze, experiment with, change, and track manpower assignments. For a sales force, tracking calls, expenses, and orders by customer and by salesperson allows a variety of sales analyses to be done and commissions to be readily computed.

Consider yourself in the role of engineering manager and take the engineering manpower plan as an example of direct application of these spreadsheet tools to budgeting. Before the budgeting process begins, you can lay out a spreadsheet for next year, with months (or weeks, if necessary) across the top and already assigned projects in the first field down the left side. From project plans, you can then assign personnel to the different projects by name and by week or month. Input the names in a way that you can sort by name to find total assignments of each person. Such a spreadsheet will give you a head start on next year's budget by showing how many new projects are needed, or can be handled, and the skills and number of people required. By doing it ahead of time, you can perhaps influence project planning for next year. When the sales and product development budgets arrive, you have a tool available to determine capacity versus the planned work load, to suggest schedule changes that can smooth peaks and valleys, to understand hiring or layoff requirements, and, finally, to budget costs.

How to Handle Your First Budget

In reducing everything to budget numbers, you must make proper use of data, trends, and models, as described in Chapter 10. For your first budget, your knowledge of any of these will probably not be extensive, so rely heavily on current-year data. Concentrate on thinking through the things that will change next year, using the information and analyses suggested in this Appendix. If there is no evident reason for change, use this year's numbers and explain to your superior that this is what you have done. This should be acceptable for your first budget; no one expects you to be an all-pro the first time.

The most fortunate new manager is the one who begins the job just as the budgeting process starts. In that case you can plead ignorance, punt on the first budget, and get away with it. Then you will have a whole year to understand the job and how to prepare the next budget.

An important thing to remember is that in any aspect of budgeting, incremental effort yields incremental benefits. Do not be daunted by the thought that a three-day session with key people, seemingly impossible because of your work load, might be required to fully understand inputs and outputs. Just one hour of private thought will lead to better understanding and better budgeting. Two hours would be twice as good. There are definite benefits from involving key people, but you should understand that any time spent studying your job and proper budgeting will be useful.

Learning the elements of budgeting is easier than learning the job skill or profession that got you the manager's job in the first place. One of the advantages of approaching budgeting as advocated here is that the things learned this way are the same ones that must be learned to be a good manager.

While learning the elements of budgeting is easy, learning how to do powerful budgeting is difficult and will take a few years. But, as a new manager, you have a few years to get there.

Index